DAD'S BOX

and
Other Fishing Stories From the Heart

by
Northwest Favorite Writer

Leonard Collins
Cover art by the Author

Dad's Old Fly Box	8
Only the Rocks Never Grow Old	24
All Alone on the River	38
When the Snow Clears	49
Kress Lake	62
Fishing as Good as the Old Days	74
The Best of Times	85
Lowe Lena Lake	95
Jefferson Lake	102
My First Steelhead	112
Getting Priorities Straight	122
Up the Clackamas River	134
Up the Clackamas River Again	143
Special and Secret Holes Revealed	156
Wilson River	164
Harriet Lake	178
The Willamette	188
Salmon Fishing in Puget Sound	201
Mukilteo	213
Funny and Weird Things on the Water	222

This book of short stories became rather special to me during this writing. At first, I thought I would merely jot down some of my fishing experiences in the northwest, but as I got into the stories I realized that I was documenting dear and personal experiences, experiences that I constantly find myself reliving over and over. It turns out that these particular happy moments are a very large part of my life. What does that say about a dreamer?

This series of short stories begins, and thereafter often dwells, somewhat, on my relationship with my father. He was a great guy, and I lead the book off with a small tribute to him.

Steelhead and salmon fishing, trout fishing, going for German brown trout, stream fishing for rainbows, high lakes fishing, and salt water fishing- it's all here.

Have fun.
I sure did.

Dad's Old Fly Box

      Finally, the time came for emptying out dad's old fly box. I could avoid it no longer. It's funny the things we put off. I guess I just wanted to prolong his life, somehow. If I didn't clean out his old box of hand-tied artificial flies, maybe he wasn't really gone? I think he would have understood my reluctance to say goodbye, but after about eighty two years, he had come to peace with his own longevity. Seeing mom, a couple sons, and all his old friends go, I'm not sure he really wanted to hang around much longer. He was tired of his own cooking.

      For about five or six years, I've been putting off all the memories stored up inside dad's old fly box. It is true that I have been avoiding the task. The box was moved from the large storage box, in the garage, to my fishing vest. I put it back. It was put on top of my work bench to remind me of my obligation. From there, the box of flies somehow was shifted over, under, and around projects all these years. Mysteriously, it ended up back in my fishing vest. Finally today, I sit here on the tailgate of dad's old truck and hold his little box of hand-tied artificial flies in his son's hands. When I unsnapped the lid, there were peals of thunder.

      When dad was still with us, and I was still a

skinny little kid, that old fly box was like the Torah, and it was always handled as if it had been one of the golden tablets fresh down the mountain. Dad had personally tied most of the flies in the box, and he had stories about a few of them that could make a young boy's head spin. Even today when I opened the box, I could almost smell the cottonwoods on the South Fork of the Skokomish River and nearly hear the clear ring of the Hansville buoy far off in the distance. One autumn afternoon, the Red Leach had turned fish in Bar Creek. The Pink Shrimp had lit up an ocean of spring salmon at Point no Point on a cold October morn, when all the other fishermen were striking out.

    Dad's old fly box holds the memories of so many good times but also brings to mind all the dumb things I did just to prove to him that I was a real man. Because dad threw a fly, I learned to fly fish, but although he was kind, I always felt his smile was merely an act of condescension. Puberty did not convince him of my manhood, so I went into the Marines- somehow that made sense, at the time. After the Marines, I became a police officer in a large metropolitan city. I don't think he was impressed, but he sure … well, yeah.., he had to be impressed, but I also think he simply thought, "Well, that's Leonard, for you! Wonder what he'll do next?" If I remember correctly, Dad started saying that about the time I entered junior high school. He would use that phrase about the same way mom would say, "I think it's just a phase Lenny is going through."

    Perhaps I was too goal oriented for dad's style of fly fishing, for I'm not a real fly fisherman. A river does not run through it. I just catch fish on artificials that I tie myself. Does that make me a fly fisherman? In reality, I don't think so. My friend, up the street, is a real fly fisherman. He builds fly rods and reels and teaches fly casting classes. Leroy travels the world teaching fly fishing and rod building. He is a real fly fisherman who ties the correct knots, and uses the prescribed thread, and the most expensive hackle material. He knows the difference between a half hitch and a couple a grannies around the eyelet of a hook. I just catch fish on artificials that I tie myself with a couple overhand knots and a glob of glue to hold it all together. Leroy won't even talk to me. When Leroy walks into the Sportsmen's Warehouse, the clerks ask what *he* can do for them. Sometimes I wonder, though, if Leroy is having *fun*. I sure am.

 Dad and I never fly fished together, but once the two of us caught a fish together on an artificial fly. I was a young boy, and dad was fishing the south fork of the Skokomish River. It would be a stretch to say we were fishing together, but it did take both of us to catch and land one wily old summer steelhead. We laughed about that fish all the rest of his life.

 I was about ten, and we were up on the Skokomish River, on the Olympic Peninsula, where Dad was fishing the large hole in front of our campsite. A wide section of shallow ripples dropped into a deep hole before the river hit some cliffs and took a harsh turn to the south. At the head of the pool, where the ripples first dropped into the hole, dad was casting a black something-or-other of which only Leroy would know the name. Dad could see a bright summer steelhead hen lying with her nose up against the ripple as the river made its first tumble into the quieter waters in front of our campsite. That fish turned up its nose at every artificial fly that dad tried. I was glued to the battle, content to watch hero casting and casting into the white frosty water at the head of the pool. After an eternity of casting, Dad came over to the side of the river and pointed the steelhead out to me.

"That's one savvy fish," he said. "You just have to admire a fish like that."

"Why?"

"Well, son, that fish is smart. I've never seen the likes. I have thrown every fly in my box at it. My presentations have been flawless, but that old fish just snubs her nose."

"Why?"

"Well, I think she just knows a natural from a piece of hair on a hook.

"How?"

He just shrugged. Then he turned from the sea-run trout to the ten-year old boy who just would not go away. "Want to help me put one over on that smart trout?" he asked.

"Oh, yeah!" He actually wanted my help. Sure. Anything. Right now! I was ten. But still latter on, after I had grown older, I maintained the same high opinion of the man and would have done just about anything he asked. I would still do anything for him when I was forty and he was.., my age, now, I guess. It must have been a difficult cross for the man to bear.

Dad tried for that steelhead hen for over an hour, and that fish ignored every offering that dad threw, but the fish was actively and aggressively feeding on legitimate insects. If even a real bug floated down the river on its own, that fish would ignore it, because the fish figured it might just be another fake fly cast by one of those weird guys who stand in the water and throw out things they think look like insects. But when a stick would come down the ripples, the fish would nose the stick over and eagerly eat anything that fell off.

This is an incredible story, I know, and I don't blame you if you think I am making it up. I think I would have made it up, if I had thought of it; it's that good. But this story is true.

Dad's idea was for me to sneak out into the ripples right above that smart, old sea-run trout and gently place an artificial fly on a small stick. The trick was to lay the fly on the stick so that the barb wouldn't sink into the wood, so the fly would fall off natural-like when the fish nosed the stick over. It was nearly impossible, and dad knew it. Most likely, the stick would get jammed in between a couple rocks and not make the trip to the pool, or the fly would fall off before the stick entered the pool, or the fish might not turn over that particular stick. The fly might not fall off the stick even if it was nudged over. Dad explained that there were just too many variables. It was a one in a million shot, he said, like shooting a dragon with a bow and arrow while standing on one foot, wearing a blindfold, in a high wind. I liked that part about the dragon. I had to try it.

As it turned out, God smiled on that little boy, and the old hero.., and also on that fresh and wily old sea-run trout. The stick floated straight and true, tumbled gently over the crest of water, and dropped into the hole. The monofilament did not get snagged, and the hook did not catch the bark of the stick. And the fish! Ah, the fish! It nosed up and turned that stick over just like we were making a movie or I was writing a book. That black fly slipped off the stick and tumbled into the water, and dad tightened the hook when he felt the pull.

Who would have figured? That old dragon fell from the sky with a thunk!

Dad clamped down on his pipe and played that fish like he played everything else in life; he let it have its own way. He gave it space while it raced up the pool throwing spray as high dad's shoulders. He played it soft when the fish took a short run downriver. That hen jumped nine times. I know it did, because I matched it jump for jump.

After about a century, the fish finally tired, and dad put a knee into the sand to bend down and gently lift the trout. She was heavy with eggs. He cradled the fish in his arms to show mom and my brothers, and then he slowly placed the fish back into the water and watched it fin back up to the head of the pool. The fish laid there for a while, exactly where it had been before all the hullabaloo about artificial flies, and sticks, and catching a steelhead on the south fork of the Skokomish River- and then it suddenly worked its way up into the riffles above the pool to resume the journey to its final destiny. Just like dad and me.

When the fish vanished, dad came over and sat on a rock next to a ten year old boy and began retying the fly that had done the dirty deed. Dad explained that the fish had been born, here, high up in the Olympic Mountains. It spent a year, or two, in the Skok and then began drifting to the sea. Eventually, the fish made its way into Hood Canal and worked against the tides all the way into the Strait of Juan de Fuca where it joined thousands of other sea-going trout to make their hearty run to the Pacific Ocean and the storied waters of Alaska. Some time in the summer, three years later, the fish turned against the current and began making its way back to the Washington coast. Somehow, that fish found the Skokomish River out of hundreds of other little streams and creeks. She ascended high up the Skokomish River to turn sticks over for insects in front of our little campsite where the river crashes into a high cliff and turns south.

"So, you see, son, after all that hard work I had to let it go, so it could spawn and make other little steelhead who will make their way down to the sea."

I must admit that I was torn. All the other trout we caught were promptly fried up over a fire. It was my first experience with gratitude and mercy on a scale nearly too big to understand. Dad said that we should turn it loose, so that it could make more fish.

"Why?"

I think he tired of explaining it to me after about the fourth time, and then he went back to fishing some little black something-or-other with a lost name.

Back in my garage, I removed about twenty little bead-head flies tied on size twenty hooks from dad's old fly box. Twenties! I can't even see the hole in the hook on a twenty. I know he used these flies, because only a man with the irritating patience of Job would do so. I remember dad telling of trout who would not even look at an artificial larger than a 20, but a twenty looks like the end of an ink pen when you click it open. It's tiny! If it was me, I would just let those fish lie and look for an easier catch, but apparently he liked challenges like fish that would scoff at anything larger than a 20 and a little boy who had always wanted to go dragon hunting.

In 1999, Dad presented me with a fly rod of my own. It was a Christmas present. Until that time, I had forgotten about fly fishing, and had been caught up in steelhead and salmon fishing with large, heavy lures in the rivers around Portland, Oregon. Reels had changed a lot, since dad's time, and I had a deuce of a time finding a fishing reel of the same type dad had used, but I finally located a Phlueger and put on a five weight floating line. Then I placed that new rod and reel in the back of my car… and left it there. Betsi asked about it, a time or two, and I always assured her that I was fixing to go fly fishing one of these days. She had no idea why I wanted to catch flies, but she didn't say anything to dash my spirits. It sounded harmless, to her, as long as I didn't bring any of those little, black, smelly things home. She said that we had enough of those things buzzing around our can by the back door, and when was I going to do anything about those obnoxious insects.

Near the end of the summer, one hot August day, Betsi and I were returning from a picnic in

Welches, Oregon, and I saw a well used place to turn out on the Sandy River. It was two in the afternoon, in bright sunlight, at a well-used turnout. And I was going to try fly fishing? Sure. Good luck.

It's not the fishing, I told her. It's the experience. She always used to just looked at me when I talked of fishing. She did not understand it. At all.

"You don't like fish."

"I love fish. I just don't like to eat them."

"Then, why fish?"

"Dad used to." That kind of reasoning did not make sense to her, but that is also why I used to elk hunt. An adult is supposed to.., because dad did that, and after a few years I grew to love the hunting experience. I never loved shooting a deer or an elk, but I loved shooting *at* them, and I enjoyed the hunt, itself, more than I could possibly express.

When Betsi and I walked down to the river, the water was low, and clear, and about twelve inches deep. All in all, those were not exactly promising fly fishing conditions.

A young man was throwing single eggs on light line. He hadn't hooked a fish in an hour, although it looked as if he knew what he was doing.

I was afraid to look at Betsi. I knew she was wondering why we had stopped at the river after a long and tiring picnic.

I tied on a #12 Royal Coachman and made my first cast. A twelve! That's huge compared to Dad's size 20- like running into a Volkswagen with a tank. But it didn't matter to those trout one little bit. I caught a trout each and every cast for half an hour! In bright sunlight! In shallow water about twelve inches deep! At the end of August! On a stretch of river that sees more fisherman than one could imagine! Betsi was awed. So was I, but I didn't let on. Fishing with the fly pole that Dad had given me was like holding onto yesterday.

Since that first day on the river, with Betsi, fly fishing has always been special for me. A great metamorphosis takes place on the first cast; I turn into a skinny kid standing on a log raft trying for six inch trout on Elk Lake.

Betsi was genuinely impressed that day on the Sandy River, and I knew that I didn't have to do anything more. That was good, because the last time I tried to impress anyone, I went into the Marines, and I sure wasn't about to try that again.

I hooked a lot of fish that hot August afternoon with Betsi standing at my shoulder watching in wonder. I guess you could say that I was hooked, also.., on a #12 Royal Coachman. I wanted to call Dad on the phone and brag to him and thank him for such a wonderful and responsive fly rod, but that's a hard call to make after he'd been gone for those five years.

As time went by, however, I began to feel that I could tie my own Coachman flies. The trouble with having an entrepreneur spirit is that you are always trying something new, always trying to improve, and I had the spirit. But spirit or no spirit- I could not tie even a #12. It was all I could do to tie a nine or ten. So I did. The size of trout flies gets larger as the number gets smaller, so a nine is huge and a twenty-four is an itty bitty tiny thing you can't hardly see.

After several clumsy attempts, I finally tied a general approximation of a Royal Coachman and laid it on the table next to one of dad's number 20s. I couldn't even see the 20s! The tank completely covered that Volkswagen.

To my surprise, the large Coachmans did not turn off the trout, at all. A larger Royal was just fine with them. Perhaps fish are just like people, everywhere? Perhaps bigger really is better? The fish just went for a number nine Coachman like it was just more food on the plate.

So, I've been fishing a Royal Coachman on a #9 hook for a few years, and I've been having more fun than a man deserves. Last year, I started tying a Modified Royal Coachman, which is really just a Coachman without trying to be too precise. With my clubby fingers, I often loose the white wings, and I'm not too careful about what I use for the tail. Lately, I've been substituting a snippet of elk hair conveniently hanging next to my tying bench instead of the prescribed hackles. I just kind of bunch 'em up and tie 'em on. A little glue works wonders. No wonder Leroy doesn't want to be my friend.

So today, in the jumble of dad's old fly box, I was surprised to find a... Royal Coachman tied on a #9 hook. I found a few of those, actually. I knew dad liked to fish the super small flies, so I wondered what those larger Royals were doing in dad's old fly box? I imagine they could have been for those few trips where he was trying for a steelhead and he needed a larger fly. But I also wonder if those number nines could have been the result of dad's eyes getting older (like mine are now). I just don't know, and I can't figure a way to ask him.

Remember Kevin Costner, in that baseball movie, asking his dad if they could have a catch? I'm going to do that, but it'll be something more like going down to the lake and casting for some live ones. I am ever confident that if that day comes, Dad won't mind throwing a fly alongside me. Hope there are steelhead in heaven.

One day long ago, dad told me about a day at Point no Point, near Hansville. Hansville is up near Whidbey Island. People often ask where Point no Point is and whether, or not, I made up the name. I tell them that it's near Whidbey Island, and then they pretend to know. From Point no Point, you can actually see downtown Seattle- way off in the distance. Seattle is just a little itty bitty speck in the distance, but it helps for people to know that Point no Point is NW of Seattle.

From our house, when we were kids, dad would just drive the one, and only, north-south road in the county until he ran out of road. That's Point no Point. About a mile more and it would be Canada.

Kitsap County is a myriad of small roads. When you grow up in a small town in the middle of nothing much but what we used call oak patch- miles and miles of nothing but underbrush with about a million miles of small blacktop roads that must all go somewhere, but *nobody* knew where all of them went. Even people who lived in Bremerton would scratch their heads and say, "Where? Point no Point? Is that a real place or a made up name?" So, really, when you can see Victoria, BC long off your port bow and downtown Seattle off your starboard.., well, you get the picture.

Dad was fond of remarking that the most fun he had ever had on the water were those days when things didn't quite work out the way he had planned, for dad was ever the self-deprecating king when it came to humor. If something funny happened to him, he just laughed about it. If the funny thing was something *he* did that was dumb enough to warrant it, he told the story at dinner time.

It seems he finally made it out to Point no Point by himself. He loved us kids, but once every great while he just wanted to go fishing, and he always said, that as much as he loved us boys, once a boy gets into the boat there is no more fishing for dad. Once in a great while, though, all alone in a boat he was in heaven.

Rented rickety old boats were lowered into the water via a long track that started high up on the dock and ran steeply down to the water. Gravity held the boat on an equally rickety old metal dolly on the track twenty feet above the water. It was like a boat teetering on a nail… on an falling aluminum ladder. We boys would sit in that boat and hold our breath, because of the height. When, finally, at the bottom of the ride, the heavy metal dolly would drop under water, and the boat would float free, and we could breath again.

That day, from the moment dad left the boat shed, he started catching silver salmon! Silvers are strange fish. Silvers are more like steelhead than dour, slow moving, uninterested king salmon. Silvers like a bait that's presented fast and furious, so dad put the Johnson into drive and was trolling so fast, that his Pink Shrimp fly was just skipping a hundred feet out back- bouncing and skidding on top of the water. The fly was intended to look like a minnow or a shrimp when deep under water. Under water, dad thought it might resemble a herring or a candle fish, but zipping along on top of the water, he had no idea what it was supposed to be. And he didn't care. The silvers loved that skipping and bouncing fly. He caught fish after fish.

Trouble is (and with salmon fishing there is always a trouble is of one kind or another), he forgot his net. Dad had left the net leaning on his old, green Oldsmobile in the parking lot. It is possible to bring many different species of fish into the boat without a net, but not a silver salmon. Dad hooked so many silvers, that afternoon, that he lost count, but he never got even one into the boat. He laughed about that all through spaghetti. The funniest thing, to dad, was that the fault had been all his, and not someone else's. He had the perfect fly, the perfect water, the perfect fish, and the perfect day. And he had a perfect time and never regretted one minute of it. You have to admire a man like that.

I sat on the tailgate of dad's old pickup truck and realized that the time had finally come for emptying out dad's old fly box. But I didn't. Sometime after the thunder died down, I folded all the cottonwoods, and the smell of the salt water and fish, and the Skokomish River into the box and snapped the lid.

I still have that Pink Shrimp in dad's old fly box, and you couldn't buy it from me for love or money. Maybe, someday, I'll go up to Point no Point when the silvers are running. But I'll take the net.

Only the Rocks

It was on the Sandy River that I learned about Eagle Creek. It changed and enriched my life as only rare beauty can. Eagle creek, and its canyon, are deep and mysterious, lovely to look at and deadly at a misstep. Its waters are both rewarding and frustrating. I love everything about Eagle Creek, but the big old rocks really irritate me, and my irritation, too, bothers me. After all, what kind of a man gets angry at rocks?

I have been standing on one particular eight foot high Eagle Creek rock for forty-one years, and while I have grown old and bent and nearly everything but my rod hand hurts, that rock has not changed one iota. Its surface is exactly as it was forty-one years ago. It's size has not shrunken. It has not moved. It has not withered or been worn down. The Indians, in my native tribe, so long ago, coined a phrase; only the rocks never change. I love that old rock. I hate that old rock. Like the rocks of the Sioux Indians, One O'clock Rock never changes. Sometimes, I think it is mutely mocking me, but at the same time I know that rock has never laughed or had a life, never married, had children, found a woman to love and cherish, and never did much but listen to Eagle Creek tumble past on its journey to the sea. It has never loved God and hated His enemies. It has never lived a life of joy, desire, frustration and rewards. It has never been loved. But on the other hand, it's never been shot at in Vietnam, beaten up by eight men and left for dead on the streets of Portland, been run over by a Plymouth station wagon and almost killed, or thrown high and free out the front door of a friendly neighborhood bar on Hawthorne Street- so maybe there's something to being a big, dumb, silent rock, after all.

About ten years ago, a heavy timber washed up on top of the rock, and we haven't had high enough waters to wash it off, since. The log has broken on both ends leaving only a twenty foot section sitting rather foolishly on top of that high craggy stone, so I can't quite climb over the log to stand where thousands of fishermen have stood for decades- whenever they beat me to it. So, I cast from behind the log and leave the spinner in the water a second longer to clear the downstream end of the log. Thankfully, the log doesn't stop me from fishing the hole, but it sure makes life more interesting. I hate that log, and there are no two ways about it. Logs aren't eternal like rocks, and I'm pretty sure that log will out live this old man. I just wish the log would wash off One O'clock Rock and outlive me someplace else.

I've thought about taking my chain saw down the canyon and cutting up that old log, but it would probably knock me off the rock, throw me in the water, and kill me. On the up side if that happened, they might change the name of the rock to Collins Rock. That would be fun, but all in all, I think I will just leave my chainsaw in the garage and cast from behind the log and leave my spinner in the water a second longer.

Before I ever saw that rock or had heard of Eagle Creek, I was on the Sandy River making a gallant attempt at catching my second steelhead, but I really had no idea. My first steelhead was lucky more than anything else, and the second was proving to be impossible. There were so many things I did not know about the fish. I was in the dark about when they ran, where they ran, how to cast, what to cast, and the task was turning out to be impossible. The first steelhead was just another snag on the bottom of the river. I yanked on the pole in frustration. It yanked back. That was fun. The first steelhead was easy. The second would not come.

On the Sandy, I met a young man once and never again. I have no idea who he was except that he was a volunteer fire fighter and had a tender spot in his heart for an equally young police officer who was frustrated over the daunting task of catching a steelhead. He had great pity on me, and he gave me a steelhead! It was his birthday, and in the space of an hour he caught two steelhead standing shoulder to shoulder with me below Tad's Chicken and Dumpling. That fire fighter watched me do everything wrong that a fisherman could do wrong and then said he had to leave and go home to his birthday party. He wished me well, told me I was retrieving my spoon too quickly, and gave me a ten pound steelhead. Just before he drove off, he told me about Eagle Creek. God bless him!

"You'll see a yellow gate along the road. Don't park there. Park one turnout before the yellow gate. Climb down into the canyon, and you will find a large rock to stand on, the largest rock in the canyon. The fish will be in the deep slot in front of the rock or sometimes the other side of the slot behind a half-size boulder sticking up out of the water."

The steelhead he gave me that cold December birthday was a very special gift, indeed, but the tip about Eagle Creek and One O'clock Rock, as I found it to be named, was nearly priceless. I found the creek exactly as the young man described it, stood on the largest rock around, and cast a steelie into the deep slot running down the middle of the creek. I couldn't see the bottom, and the slot proved to be snaggy, snaggier than under the bridge at Dodge Park, and that is saying something. The water was dusty green, about the color of an avocado, but it shined and glittered gold where the sun hit.

I stood on that big, old rock and cast into the dark waters for an hour. I lost ten rigs, if I lost one. Touch the bottom, and the lure would stick like glue. I was going broke at break neck speed. Then, surprise on surprise! As my spoon drifted down the far edge of the slot, I saw the flash of a large fish turn from its hiding place and follow the spoon. The fish hurried past the spoon and took it in the deep water at the end of the slot. And what a fish! It jumped twice in the slot and took off down river like it had just remembered something important near sea level. I jumped twice on the rock in front of the slot and took off down river like I had remembered something important. Only much slower than the fish.

As snaggy as that hole is, it is also treacherous. I thought it difficult climbing *up* onto the rock, but trying to hurry down off it, while holding a running and jumping steelhead, was a nightmare. And hurry I had to do. If I couldn't get below that fish and put pressure on it from down river it would spill over the bottom of the hole and rush with the heavy current to a no man's land of slippery rock, no bank, fast water, and a nightmare of a chase. But if I could get below the fish and put pressure on it from down river, the fish might just turn away from the pressure of the hook and go up river and return to One O'clock where tiring it out and bringing it in to the shore might just be possible. But One O'clock Rock sits on top of other high rocks, and it just took too much time to climb down- and that was when I was young and agile.

    That fish, however, was younger and agiler- if you will allow that word. That fish was gone.

    Well, not quite gone. To a sane man, it would have been gone. How do you say crazy in Sioux Indian? I don't know that word, but I know that fish was yatahay- gone like the wind. When that word is exclaimed, you are supposed to slap your open left palm with your right hand and quickly thrust your right arm towards the horizon and exclaim, "Yatahay!" I am a descendant of a Sioux Indian Princess, and I know these things. I saw it in a John Wayne movie.

    Luckily, the fish paused for a few minutes at the foot of the hole. His pause allowed me to climb down from One O'clock Rock, scramble down the other, smaller rocks, and catch up with him where four smaller stones step out into the river. The fish thrashed as only a large, heavy fish can thrash. My heart beat rapidly as only a young man's heart can with impunity. The fish rested for a few moments in the foot of the pool and then calmly dropped over the lip of the tail out into the fast chute of water below. I was crazy to follow. Got to look up *that* Indian word.

Below One O'clock Rock, there is no bank, no trail, no way to follow an errant, wild, jumping steelhead trout. The saving grace was that when the fish decided to drop downriver it was on my side of a huge boulder mid river. If it had gone on the other side, this story would be much shorter. The fish ran like the wind. I hit the free spool.

A month before this second steelhead of mine, an article in *Salmon Trout and Steelhead* advised that for a running steelhead, set the reel on free spool, so the tension would slacken on the fish and he might slow down or stop- the theory being that the fish was running from the pressure of the hook, and if the pressure could be taken away he might settle down snug behind a rock or in a deep pool of cool water. I tried it, but on free spool, you would be amazed at how quickly line runs off a bait casting reel- all the time while I was searching for a handhold on the canyon wall.

There was no hand hold, but there were a few tree roots coming out of the vertical wall of mud and sandstone that make up the cliff face. I grabbed a root, found a one-inch outcropping of mud for my foot, and climbed out onto the impassable cliff above the fast water a mere foot below. It was foolhardy. It was that unknown Indian word, again, but, somehow, I found a way across the cliff to a small gravely outcropping.

It was amazing; on free spool, the fish acted just like the magazine article said he would. He stopped, mid river, just as I had hoped. The fish jumped a couple more times when I tightened up on him, but I could see that he was tiring. I jumped a couple more times and pulled him onto the gravel. When he was lying half submerged, and we were both panting for breath on the gravel, I casually took in my surroundings, analyzed the situation, weighed my options, became aware of the beauty around me.., and pounced on that fish like a man on a greased pig. It must have been a sight!

I could not find even a trace of a way back on the cliff to get back up to One O'clock Rock. To this day, I don't know how I followed that fish! It was an incredible act of bravery, fortitude, and daring. It was that Indian word.

That was my second steelhead. My second steelhead was not really the one the volunteer fire fighter gave me, but the fish I chased down the canyon.

The canyon shuts out most of the sun, most of the time, most of the year. Get the picture? It is a dark canyon with a creek fifty feet wide. Mostly, it is a shallow little creek running a foot or two deep with a good deep hole every couple hundred feet. The fish dart and hide between holes and bury themselves in deep water to rest up, when the can. That's where one finds steelhead in Eagle Creek- hiding in the depths or behind rocks that kick up a little current and hide them from the sunlight. Which rock they are lying behind, is a secret known only to God- who likes men to do their own research, but perhaps that's the fun of it. The fish lie in different spots at different water heights. If a man doesn't know where the fish are likely to be when the water rises a foot, he can fish the usual places without much success. It was like that the day a man begged me for my steelhead.

My heart always catches when I round the corner and get the first glimpse of the pullout- not at the yellow gate but the turnout before the gate. If it's full of cars, I know it will be difficult to get onto the rock- so I wince and count the cars along the road. Sometimes, a man will claim that rock and just fish there for hours and hours. Once I saw a man plunking in the slot! It was like wearing a cowboy hat into church. All the time the plunker was there, I felt as if the hole was being violated. I fished for two hours in the little slot downriver. That little slot is non-productive. I've never seen a fish in it, never caught a fish in it, and never talked to anyone who had, but I wanted my time on One O'clock Rock and just kept casting and casting and not watching my line at all- I just kept staring at the plunker. I gave him the evil eye every way I could think, and still he remained. Finally, I gave up and went up to the park to fish the spillway.

There was a fish in the spillway- a large ten pound bright fish with heavy pink along his sides. He took under the lip of the raceway and headed down river. So did I. That bank is like heaven. To begin with, there *is* a bank, and it is populated with small rocks a man can walk on, with sandy little beaches a man can pull a fish up onto, and with no overhanging branches to get in the way of a man reeling in a fish. I like catching fish at the spillway, but it has only happened twice, in forty years, so I usually give it a half a dozen casts and then walk up to the corner hole.

    The next day there were half a dozen cars at the pull out. And there were half a dozen fishermen in the canyon. They were all over the hole fishing the weirdest places, places where a fish has never been found, places where no self respecting steelhead would ever be, places that did not make sense. I walked down to the river bed, smiled, nodded, and took in the situation. The water was a foot higher than optimum. There were no fish on the bank or hanging in the tree next to One O'clock Rock. There was only one spot open to fish, one rock with nobody standing on it- the one rock where the fish were most likely to be when the water was a foot high! I couldn't believe my luck. Those guys were all fishing the wrong places. Even the ones fishing the slot would most likely not connect in water of that height. Where the fish were when the water was a foot high, was off the only rock available to me. Tough luck, that.

    I put on a medium sized spin-n-go because the water is only a foot deep on the other side of the river just below a dark brown snagy piece of sandstone just under the surface. It doesn't look like much, but the bottom of the streambed drops a little, there, and the fish in higher water don't have to fight the current as much as they would in the slot below One O'clock Rock. I took my time tying on. I smiled a couple more times and nodded when anyone caught my eye. Then I put my first cast spot on above the dark brown snagy rock and immediately tightened up the line to keep the spin-n-glo just off the bottom but still floating down river on the current. When it dropped behind the brown rock, I dipped my pole minutely and was immediately into a large and brightly colored steelhead that jumped six times and ran up river instead of down- which is kind of like saying hello to a red headed woman at closing time who smiles at you instead of smirking. I mean, with the smirk it might still be doable, but you better get your make on right away because that show is nearly over, before it begins. I have no personal knowledge of redheaded women in bars at closing time, of course, but I have hooked a few steelhead behind that brown rock, and it sure helps when the fish smiles and runs *up* river instead of dropping down and over the tail of the pool into the fast chute below.

    The fish smiled, ran up above One O'clock Rock, and settled behind the two small boulders that mark the head of the pool. I was content to let it sulk, there, as long as it wanted, because every minute it stayed there and fought against the pull of the line was another minute it burned up energy- and a tired fish will most likely not run down and out of the pool. After a minute, the fish with the smile jumped once, and nosed up out of the head of the pool, but when it felt the faster current above the pool it returned to where it had snuggled up behind the rocks. It lacked the fight and speed of a fresh fish. It was tiring, so I put pressure on the fish by raising the tip of the pole and clamping down on the spool. The fish turned on its side, and all I had to do, then, was continue pulling it over to the bank. I dispatched the fish with a rock that could have been used by my cousins for a thousand years to dispatch fish at the foot of One O'clock Rock.

There is a branch in a fir tree on the downriver side of One O'clock Rock. The branch is clean and smooth and has a neat little upturn like a hook on the end and has held many a steelhead for many a fisherman who was lucky enough to hook a fish with a smile. Few things are as dear to my heart on a lovely and cold December morning with a frost in the air, with the golden sun breaking through the branches and lighting the water with pixy sparkles, with a delightful sweet smelling fire burning on the bank.., few things are dearer to me- than seeing a dead fish hanging in the tree below One O'clock Rock.

I hung the fish and went back to my fishing, but there did not seem to be another fish behind the brown snagy rock across the river.

After making my fifth or sixth cast, a man came up behind me and asked if he could have my steelhead. I had never heard that, before. I shook my head and continued casting to the brown snagy rock.

"I'll buy it," he offered. "I'll give you twenty dollars for it?"

"No," I replied rather firmly. "That fish is not for sale."

He began to whine. "But I'm staying at my brother-in-law's, and it would sure impress him if I could bring a fresh steelhead home."

"No," I repeated.

He kept whining and begging for a few minutes, until I began to fear he was about to get violent. He had moved in right behind me, and was in the way of my casting, so I turned around and spoke harshly to him, but I wish I hadn't. "You better take off, pardner. I'm not selling that fish to you. Leave me alone, and get out from behind me!"

Wasn't that marvelous of me? Some poor guy valued that fish more than his dignity and begged me for it, and I got self righteous and yelled at him. It was the manly thing for me to do; it was macho, but hadn't someone once given me a steelhead? And hadn't I lied and told the kids that I had caught it? Given the chance all over, I would have given the fish away and walked with him all the way to his car. I might have made a friend, there.

Another time, I did give a steelhead away-from the same identical rock. Mark Wold and his brother, Jay, and I were over on the Sandy trying to catch a steelhead with absolutely no luck when I suggested Eagle Creek. Funny I would do that? We found the creek a foot high, so I went immediately to that brown snagy rock and hooked a small but bright little buck. The fish thrashed and tried to run, but I held it and forced it up into the slot where I could let it simmer down. When the fish came to the beach, I beat it up with another ancient river rock and gave it to Jay. His eyes went wide. That sounds pretty nice, but giving it away meant that I did not have to clean it, I did not have to mark it down on my tag, and I did not have to eat fish. All in all, not a bad bargain.

It was on the Sandy River that I learned about Eagle Creek. It changed and enriched my life as only rare beauty can. Eagle creek and its canyon are deep and mysterious, lovely to look at and deadly at a misstep. Its waters are both rewarding and frustrating. I love everything about Eagle Creek.

All Alone on the River

The wife was visiting in-laws in LaGrande, so I rolled out of bed before first light to go fishing. Rolling out of bed is actually overstating it. I'm sixty-four now, so.., but no- on second thought.., rolling might be pretty spot on. I sure can't spring out of bed since my springer got bent, so rolling off the edge of the bed is about the only way I *can* manage that little maneuver. I have perfected this cute little way that is really more of a freefall where I end up on my feet if all goes right. If the freefall doesn't quite work out, it leaves me kinda running and falling towards the doorway while trying to catch my feet. The wife doesn't suspect a thing. A sixty-four year old man running to the bathroom in the middle of the night. That's news?

I have been in combat for my country, and I have spent my share of time in a patrol car for my city. Both tend to take the complaining out of a man, and I really am not complaining about getting up in the middle of the night. I am thrilled to be sixty four. I'm thrilled to have, so far, avoided the only other option. I am also thrilled to be going fishing at first light on Eagle Creek.

Eagle Creek is a special place. It used to be highly popular, nearly impossible to find a rock another fisherman wasn't already on, and at the same time, highly rewarding. I really do not know how many fish I have caught in Eagle Creek, through the years. Isn't that amazing! But I guess it's just not that popular a creek, anymore, because lately I have had the canyon to myself and have only seen a couple other fishermen even up in the park. Of course, there are not the fish there used to be, and that is a big factor in the number of fishermen, but I think it might be the sixty-four year old thing again. A whole lot of my contemporaries took the other option way too early, and young men aren't taking up fishing like they used to, when I was a boy. If they do, they buy a big boat and hit the Willamette. God bless them for that!

Fishermen give up on Eagle Creek way to early in the year. Tomorrow will be April 21st, and most people will be on the Willamette trying for salmon or at Cedar Creek on the Sandy stacking up for spring salmon stacking up below the hatchery. But it is true that Eagle Creek holds fish way through June. I don't know how it continues to have steelhead when all the other rivers and creeks have dried up; I just know that I have caught fish through the first part of June! June!

One fine June day, I was carrying a particular fish up to the car, and a man began yelling at me. It was his decided opinion that I should not have kept that steelhead, because it was not a proper Eagle Creek fish. It was his opinion, he voiced very loudly, that my fish was a Clackamas River steelhead, and that I should not have kept it because the poor fish just came up Eagle Creek to get some fresh water to clean out it's gills. To tell you the truth, I did not understand him then, and I don't understand him, now. So? It's a fish! I would have kept it on the Clackamas, if I had caught it there.

When I awoke that morning, I did that roll out of bed thing pretty good, grabbed on my clothes and left the house while my socks were still getting warm in my shoes. Leaving the house in the dark of night always reminds me of running out the door for a midnight watch to drive a police car. That was a fun job. I'd still rather be doing that any chilly morning than fishing.

The morning was cool, but the donut helped. I don't recommend donuts in the morning. I sure don't. But you have to remember that sixty-four thing. This old body doesn't *want* to get going in the morning. I once had an old Dodge pick-up truck just like me. If I didn't give it a shot of starting fluid, in the morning, it wasn't very reliable. Pray for my back pain, and I'll quit taking those shots of donut. Maybe. But then the ethics of the thing will get in the way. If prayer works for my back- and I am absolutely sure that it does- then two fixes are better than one. Does excommunicated have one x or two?

I drove without stopping until I got to the Eagle Creek corner where I pulled in and got some hot coffee and an authentic donut. I didn't say anything, but I was tempted; a few years ago, the striking blond that used to work behind the counter died in Eagle Creek on a cold and icy morning when her car slid off the road. That was one single tragedy! Good things usually have bad sides to them, and even a beautiful river is not a lot different than other things in this life. Ask the old man found floating just below One O'clock Rock. If I remember correctly, he was as old as me- and he had no business being down in that canyon all alone before it was even light. He should have known better.

I thought about him as I bumped my head on that troublesome tree across the steps leading down into the canyon. If I had waited for first light, I guess I would have seen it and avoided a head bump, but it's only been there about ten years, and I'm not quite used to it yet, and I have bumped my head about a dozen times even in bright sunlight. I usually, as a matter of tradition, bump my head, give it a little Marine Corps jargon, and drop down the trail to One O'clock Rock.

There was nobody on One O'clock Rock. (What a surprise at five in the morning?) The really good news was that I did not spill the coffee. I found my donut right where I had stashed it in my fishing vest- except that when I went to fish it out of my vest, I found it all flattened up against the tube of shrimp oil.

With nothing else to do, I sat on that great big log that washed up on top of the rock when Ronald Reagan and Margaret Thatcher were taking on Russia. If daylight was coming slowly on the road where I parked my car, down in the canyon it was dragging its feet. When you hold your donut up to the sky and cannot even see the hole, there is just no way you can tie on a spinner. That's a rule that borders right on being a law. So, I waited. I'm not good at waiting, and each hour I checked my watch, there was still a half hour until fishing time.

Now, I've fished that hole some, since 1976, or so. People my age can't ever quite be sure of such dates back into antiquity, but it was at least ten years before the Ronald Regan thing and the mystical appearance of the log on top of the rock. I waited. All I really needed for fishing the slot was a faint hint of a glow in the sky. If I could see the water, I could hit that slot in front of the rock. I didn't need much help, but that donut was really not cooperating.

Then it happened. One minute I could not see the last guide on the Lamiglas, and the next I was hitching 'em up and getting ready for my first cast. That lob was perfect. The spinner touched the bottom, and I tightened up, slightly, to keep it spinning and moving as the current propelled it dead straight down river on its way through the slot. It bumped three times, and I lifted the tip to take the spinner over a rock. I cannot tell you how many spinners I have left on that snag. If the river ever dries up, I'm going down there and get back a few hands full of metal off the bottom of that creek.

Nothing hit the first pass through, so I tried it again. Here it comes- Whammo!!!!

Now, while it is true that it was passable light to cast, it sure was not light enough for a frantic scramble down off that rock! That is a difficult maneuver in the daylight. Trying it by Braille was an experience not for the faint at heart and not to be tried at home! That is probably what happened to the seventy year old man. That rock is eight feet high, and it sets on top of other six foot high rocks. Those rocks are craggy where you want them smooth and smooth where you want a foot hold. I made it, but every time I make that mad scramble, I think it takes a mite longer to unfold when I reach the bottom. Now that I'm older and a mite slower, when I finally jump down and start to get a little line back, the fish, it seems, have been farther down the hole than they used to be.

It is essential, at One O'clock Rock to get below a running fish before it drops down to the tail out. It is imperative to somehow get below the fish and put pressure on it from down river. That way, a savvy fish will turn and begin working up river away from the pressure of the hook. It's supposed to work that way. It's in all the magazines. Luckily, this fish had read all the latest *Salmon Trout and Steelheader,* because darned if that old fish did not swim right back up into the slot and try to return to the same place he had been before I was so rude as to put a hook into him. That was fine with me. I've chased fish downriver from One O'clock Rock, and I don't want to ever do that again. It's cliff and mud and slippery and dangerous all the way, and when you get there you just have to climb back up when the fight is all over.

I put pressure on the hook, again, from down river- not much just enough so that the fish would not camp in the slot. There is, from time to time, some hundred pound mono from kind souls who fish with that junk, and it's just terminal to come into contact with it when you throw ten pound mono from the Sportsman's Warehouse. Dan wrapped the line onto my brand new, shiny Ambassador reel when I purchased it last month, and he didn't charge me for the line, so I guess this plug pays him back, but it might also get him fired for the freebie. When I pulled, the fish tailed pretty powerfully up into the water above the rock across the creek and settled into the calmer water where it first spills into the hole. I knew from the way his tail wagging was slowing, that the fight was ending, so I began a slow, but deliberate, line pull. He didn't want to, but he came in. When the fish was nearly at my feet, I sensed when the time was just perfect and swiftly swooped the tip of the pole over towards dry land. The fish followed. When his head touched the shallow rocks, he became alarmed, but because his head was pointing out of the water his tail wagging only pushed him further up and out of the water. A fish finds it impossible to back up, so if it is already started out of the water and flops its tail- that fish is going up onto dry land. This one did. I mashed it with an Indian Hammer.

    I hung that fish in the tree at the base of One O'clock Rock and settled back to mark my steelhead tag. Once that was done, I climbed back onto the rock and set my pole down. Then I climbed up onto the tall side of that snag and fidgeted in my vest until I found dad's old pipe and some old, dried up tobacco. Betsi wasn't around, so I lit that pipe and sat up on the old tree and blew blue all over that river. I reveled in my success in the bright and clear morning, thought about all the good times I had experienced in that canyon, and then my thoughts started straying to the owner of the pipe, the original owner of the pipe.

    He was a pretty marvelous guy, my dad, and I sure miss him. Sometimes, I hear him in my brother Wesley's humor, but mostly I just miss him being around when I need him. I think that is a tribute to him, that his sons miss him and never wish that he'd been different but that we would just all like to see him back, again, just like he was. He took us in, we boys, when he married our mum, and when mom left we just stayed right there. It seemed like the right thing to do. And it was. So, every year, I pull out that old pipe and light up. That was just about how old the tobacco was, too, so pretty quickly I knocked the fire out on that old tree and began examining the slot some more.

One snowy Christmas morning below One O'clock Rock, I met a young man in a brown cowboy hat. He was leaving for Iraq the next morning. Hope he made it. He struck out on the steelhead that morning. I wished him godspeed and watched him walk away into the woods- just like others had watched me leave for Vietnam about a hundred years before.

I took several additional casts, but lightning just wasn't about to strike twice in the same place, that morning, so I turned and cast down to shallower water across the creek just in front of a little sandstone outcropping. I love this part- Whammo! That's not quite accurate, though; the fish hit softly, just tugging on the line as if he had put his mouth around something sharp and he would like to spit it out. He had. He didn't. He jumped twice and came to the gravel. So did I.

Now, I am sixty-four years old. Did I mention that? It is no small job for my waders to climb up that canyon wall when all they have is me, my fishing pole, and my six shooter. With two fish, it was quite a burden. There is no cute little way to fall up that canyon, and I was head down struggling to make the climb when my top knot hit that tree across the trail.., again. I hope God forgives me for what I called that innocent old piece of wood.

    I had hoped to fish the Corner Hole and then go over to the Sandy and fish Dodge Park, but my plans sure went awry when I had to turn the truck around and drive home. A limit of steelhead can ruin an otherwise fine morning. I went home early, and to tell you the truth I was a little tired. After all, Truman was president when I was born.

    I have spent my share of time in a patrol car for the city, and being in a patrol car again is about the only thing I would rather do than fish another day on Eagle Creek.

When the Snow Clears

When the snow clears, and the road is finally passable, and it seems that we cannot wait another week- Betsi and I push our way up to our favorite high mountain lake. I say push our way, because early in the season the road still has dark, shady corners where the snow threatens the bottom of our old rusty Subaru. That dirt road is usually pitted with deep pot holes early in the season, so when we are not fording through the snow, we are bouncing like a greenhorn at the Pendleton Roundup. Later on in the summer, Skamania County will grade the road, but early in the season the road is a tad rough- as in kiss your kidneys goodbye, because a Subaru is not smooth on pavement; on a pothole covered road, a Subaru is Murder One. The next morning, my back always kills me, but the pain is offset by remembering the blue and green water, the bald eagles, and the osprey... and about thirty German brown trout eager to rise to my home-made fly. You see, an old man's life is mainly made up of two things- memories, back pain, and two trips a night to the bathroom. It's also been about fifty years since I took a class in addition, and I was educated in a public school, so I'm not sure if that's two things that are paramount in an old man's life or four.

For about forty years, I chased steelhead and salmon constantly on the search for larger fish, a bigger trophy, a monster that I could brag about the next day at the station. It seemed the cops, in my precinct, could be neatly divided into two groups; those who fished and those with whom I seldom met for coffee. The second group always wanted to talk cop shop- who is wanted on the district, who killed the man on the corner, the latest and newest law- and I just shunned that kind of talk, if I could. It always seemed to me, as I rode around in my patrol car, that there just were not enough fishing tackle stores in southwest Portland. My interests seemed to be centered on chasing large, strong, twenty pound steelhead and fifty pound salmon. I arrested people for a living. I fished, because I was addicted. I wrote a book about my police work, *Portland Police Stories*. Did that read like a plug?

Since my retirement, and in what some might call my declining years, I have returned to my roots; for I now love fishing the quieter waters as I did when I was a boy on Kitsap Peninsula and in the Olympic Mountains. *Catching* fish means a lot less to me, now, than when I was younger and healthier, and I am embracing my new reality as a good thing. Perhaps, it's just a pain thing? Rowing a kayak around a high mountain lake just kicks my butt less than crawling all day long over slippery rocks on the Clackamas River. Catching has been replaced by the experience.

Betsi and I are searching for memory makers- for warm days, quiet blue water where we can watch the eagles, spot an occasional deer or elk grazing on the shore, or marvel at the brutal splash of an osprey on the hunt. Fishing has turned into a hunt for my youth- catching pan-sized trout with dad, and Tommy, and Wesley. Those were the good old days, but I just can't seem to find them. I keep looking for that old man with the wildly crooked nose lighting his pipe and smiling from ear to ear when one of us would hook a really good one, but I haven't found him yet- except once I thought I caught a glimpse of him when I leaned over to look deep into the water. For a second, I thought I saw him then, but it turned out only to be my own reflection in the water. Perhaps in some mirror universe, dad was looking over the side of his boat wishing he could see one of us boys. That would have startled him! I don't quite look like I did when he was around. But it's a fun thought, nonetheless.

    Dad and we boys caught a lot of little planted fish in the lakes surrounding Kitsap County. Millions of 'em. In my adult life I could never do that. Somehow the magic of it wore off, and I had to settle for the total experience in place of fish. I kept telling Betsi I was a fisherman, and she kept believing me, but as the years went by- even I, myself, wondered at my memories. Finally, I just decided to settle down and enjoy the experience (which is what one always says when one can't catch a fish to save his life). Out of desperation, I settled for a new goal- slow down and enjoy myself, settle for a fish now and then, and pretend that the very occasional fish is okay and satisfying. Take pictures of the lake. Write a book about fishing.

    But what if we could have all those memories, all those slow, wonderful, relaxing summer days in an idyllic setting *and* catch an amazing amount of large, jumping, vicious fish? Without moving to Alaska. Would not that be like heaven-on-a-stick?

    I figure that God looked down on Betsi and me, one day, flicked his little finger, and said, "Why not just give them a little present? Just a present- from Me to them. Just for the fun of it." And he gave us *our* lake. John Gierach would call it finding our home water, but the lake is a little far away from Milwaukie to actually call it home.

    This last June, I think both Betsi and I were a little surprised when we parked the car and found the lake exactly like we left it, begrudgingly, the previous October. When, again, I stood on the shore and stared at the lake, it confirmed that it had not been just a wonderful dream, that we really had found our secret water in the woods, our Valhalla, our.., well I guess we could call it our home water, after all. It sure felt that way.

    It was windier than we liked it, but wind comes and goes on a high mountain lake, and the north end, by the reeds and tall grass, is usually out of the wind, so we launched with smiles, great anticipation, and some sun block.

    I think Betsi was a little disappointed when I immediately laid out the five weight line and one of my home-tied flies instead of rowing along side-by-side for the first ten minutes, so I returned the pole under its bungi and took my position to her right. That first ten minutes is the mood setter. She smiled when I came up beside her kayak. The wind died, and the water turned its characteristically blue-green reflecting the high mountain alpine trees and white dead snags along the bank. Right off, a bald eagle buzzed us. Puffy, white clouds hung in a royal blue sky. Betsi's smile has that effect on things

A few minutes later, at the north end- where a dead snag points out into the lake- I finally spun the kayak and laid fifty feet of yellow line behind the boat. The fly was the same Royal Coachman Modified that had caught trout at Kress Lake a few weeks earlier, and it's always best to lay out a tried and true pattern to take the jinx out of the boat.

Right off, there was a small tug but nothing hooked, so I waited a few seconds and then rowed on. Perhaps the slight twitch on the line was simply a piece of grass or a missed take by a smallish trout. I have seen fish take a swipe at the fly and miss or just catch the tail hackles. It could have been that, I told myself. Often, the fish that misses will come back and hit again, so I usually get real excited and pay attention for a few minutes before lapsing back into my daydreams.

Ten minutes later, there was a large swirl and the line tightened. The fish played true to German brown modus operandi; it hit hard and jumped twice. Then it ran for the boat. That's the tricky part; it is difficult to keep the line tight when a large fish runs for the boat. The typical fly reel is not a fast retrieve, so I reel as fast as I can, but it's seldom fast enough, and one can only try. Reeling so fast always makes me feel like one of those bass fishermen on television; they hook a fish, yell whoopee, and reel as fast as their five-to-one retrieve system can crank. That doesn't look like fun. Trying to keep up with a wild, thrashing, brown trout is.

Most browns in our lake don't start really fighting until they see the boat, and some not until they see the net. Then it breaks out! It's fun, but alarming, when a ten inch heavy bodied fish goes aerial hard up against the kayak. By some whim of fate, their ferocious display usually waits until I get to the miss-tied splice where the fly line meets the leader. For all of last season, I meant to retie that splice. It's been the worst splice I have ever tied, and if I reel in past that troublesome splice it's sometimes difficult to let out line again when a fish demands it by a heavy run away from the boat. I would fix that splice, but usually I don't think about until it's time to load the kayaks and head for home, and then I am always in a hurry to get on the road. When we get home, it's time to unload the boats, so the car can fit into the garage.

So this time, just like last time I hooked a fish, when I tried to swing the net on the fish there was too much line out, and I couldn't reach the fish. One intelligent solution would be to cut a foot or so off that leader and fix the splice while I'm there, but somehow it hasn't gotten done. That's what I've been meaning to do for about a year, now, but usually when I think of it, I'm in my robe, and I haven't been able to find my slippers for about the same length of time that the splice has been bad, and the concrete floor is cold in the garage. That knot has, somehow, just stayed as big and unwieldy as it's ever been. And the leader has remained two feet two long. Of course, I *could* retie that splice and chop a couple feet of length off that leader while out on the lake, but that's prime fishing time, and I just can't seem to take the line out of the water for such trivialities.

It was a treat to watch a healthy brown trout jump and jump and jump six feet from the boat with my heart in my throat all the time the aerial display was going on. Finally, the fish tired, and my heart settled, and I brought the fish to the net. I would have turned it back into the crystal clear water, but Linda's birthday was the next day, and she sure loved trout. Nevertheless, dropping that trout into the creel made me feel just a bit guilty.

I met a man in a pontoon boat, that morning, who said that my method of trolling a fly was not really fly fishing. Fly fishing, he advised, was casting to rises or likely looking water. I countered that I don't have any down-time with my method, that most of his fishing time was taken up in back casts and waving his bright, new fishing pole back and forth through the cool, mountain air. My method, I said, puts the fly in the water all the time. His conclusion was that he was right, and that I was wrong. Could be?

For the next two hours, Betsi explored the north end of the lake. She plowed her blue and white kayak up the little intake stream just as far as possible. She always returns from such errands with a smile and a story. "You should see the numbers of fish up that creek!" I learned a long time ago not to take those kind of stories too seriously. Oh, I know that Betsi was serious, and that there were too many fish up that creek to shake a stick at, but somehow whenever I have followed up leads, like that, the fish all went away, or they wouldn't bite for love or money.

For the next two hours, I missed strike after strike. Most of them were small, so I didn't feel too sad about missing their strikes, but I did go to a size twelve Royal Coachman that I bought from some gentleman on ebay. Unfortunately, even after switching to the smaller flies, I continued missing strikes, so I tied my larger modified back on. I figured that if I was going to miss all the strikes in the world, I might as well do it on my own creation.

A couple days earlier, I had tied a scant few elk hairs horizontally across a number eight light hook and put some red behind it. For a tail I wound a few threads around the last half inch of a light, brown feather Betsi and I had found on Centennial Lake in Beaverton. It looked good.., to me. Fishing on the lake with Betsi, it looked pretty much like one of the dead mosquitoes floating on the surface- except that it would be the largest dead mosquito any of those fish would ever see.

The fish didn't mind too much about the size. Perhaps fish aren't as smart as we think they are, or maybe they like their meals supersized just like we do. It was only a few minutes before a large swirl engulfed that oversized mosquito. I let the fish tug for a two count and then lifted the rod up. Predictably, the fish gave a jump at the rod pull and then made a run for the boat. I hate that. I love that. It ran right up to the boat, and the line went slack.

Betsi came over and consoled me over the loss of what looked to be a pretty good fish, but the fly did not pop up to the surface, and that made me wonder if I really had lost the fish? I raised the tip of the rod as high as it would go, and the leader billowed in the wind, but I still could not see my fly. "Yep. You lost that fish," she said. "That's a fish that isn't!"

"Then why?" I answered, "isn't the fly flopping in the wind?" It dawned on me, nearly too late, that that fish was doing the best imitation of a lost fish that I have ever seen, he was lying directly under the boat where the tension from the that dumb mosquito's hook was the slightest.

"I don't think I lost this one," I said, and reeled up past that troublesome splice. Of course, as soon as I reeled in a couple feet of line, that fish came alive like he had set a trap and had done all that hiding under the boat stuff before- to some other dumb fisherman. Finally, after a moment or two of heart stopping tugging and pulling, the splice worked it's way back through the fishing pole's last eyelet, and I let the fish run. After a pretty encouraging run, the fish that wasn't came to the net.

I learned early on with browns, to fold the net over, because if one thinks they fight hard in the water- wait until you lift them up in the net! Bazooka! (We used to say that as kids, and I've always wanted to put that in a story.) A wild and thrashing trout can leap clear out of a net, leave the best tied artificial fly stuck in the netting, and swim away laughing.

As I worked the fly loose from his toothy lip, that cagey old fish bit me, and I guess that was fair enough. I watched, as the fish that wasn't, but was, swam away and became the fish that still is. Perhaps we will meet again. In time, he will likely forget the look of my Modified Royal Coachman that looks, to me, like a sick, dead, deteriorating mosquito, and that brown might just come out to play again.

This lake, this home water that is two hours away from our actual hearth and home and mortgage- this highly beautiful and thrilling lake- where a man who simply trails a hook with a feather on it will consistently hook thirty, or more, broad backed, deep bellied, wild brown trout. This lake holds a special place in our hearts. I will never keep another fish caught out of her depths, I will never, again, kill a fish from that treasure of the Gifford Pinchot National Forest. Such wonderful fish, in such a rare and beautiful lake, deserve to have another chance at life, and love, and living. In the cool depth of a high mountain lake that each one of those browns believe to be *their* home waters, they are really something to behold. I will not kill another fish from *our* lake.
    Unless it's a really big one.

    Early in the afternoon, I decided to quit fighting the light breeze that sprang up and just drifted the length of the lake letting the wind push me along, for whenever possible, I am a lazy fisherman.
    When I was a boy in Puget Sound, fishing for salmon with my dad and brothers, we used to call it mooching; we would just drift along with the wind and the current and let our herring bounce along on the bottom. On the lake, I could trust the wind to keep the fly line tight, so all I had to do was a modified mooch and watch the eagles and ospreys. Halfway across the lake I noticed a large spider had found a home on the kayak, so I flicked him into the water. I marveled when he landed on all twelve legs and sat high and dry on the surface film like my home made

flies refuse to do. My usual method is to keep out fifty or sixty feet of fly line and try to be quiet and sneaky, so I don't upset the fish, so when a large gulp engulfed that high bobbing spider- not three feet from the boat- I just had to laugh.

About that time, the sun started going behind the trees. When the sun leaves the water on a high mountain lake, a couple things happen at once; it begins to get cold, so Betsi heads for the boat ramp, and the fish start rising all over the lake. I usually pretend to follow Betsi towards the take-out, but how do you leave the water just when the good times begin to roll?

In the middle of the lake are the remains of an ancient forest, and the white snags stick up about ten feet. Sparrows have drilled about a hundred little homes in the snags, and it's fun to be in the middle of the snags with all those swallows swooping back and forth catching midges, and all those fish rising and jumping to catch their own midges. I was sitting still, in the middle of that dead forest, when I started hearing the strangest sounds- like a high pitched chirping. I turned and looked at Betsi, who was far away and watching an eagle in a tree near the take out. There were no trucks at the boat launch playing music. Then I noticed the sounds were coming from a hole in one of the trees. A swallow was feeding its chicks, and the sound I had heard was the pleading, and low chirping, and cuddling sounds the chicks made while being fed. That was pretty much worth the trip, right there.

Finally, the cold began getting to Betsi, and we both started for the ramp to load up the boats and plow our way through the snow up high on the pass. It was time to head for home. We promised each other to return in a few days if our work load let us., and once again we will plow through the deep snow on the shadowy corners and bounce along on the pot holes.

When the snow clears, and the road is finally passable, and it seems that we cannot wait another week- Betsi and I will push our way up to our favorite high mountain lake. My back will be sore the next morning, but I won't care.

Bazooka!

Kress Lake

Kress is a little known lake near Kalama, Washington. It's easy to get to, just off Interstate 5, and has great access. And it's a good lake. True, it's not a remote high mountain lake that takes several hours over dirt roads, but it's a good little lake to fish. Most people who fish Kress are plunkers who mostly retrieve the standard fare; eight to ten inch rainbows from the stocking truck. But if you have a boat.., well, the whole world of fishing changes when you have a boat- any boat. There is a good boat launch, albeit gravel, and once onto the surface of the water you can pull away from the bank fishermen pretty fast. It's not a high mountain lake, but it is surrounded by trees and a day on Kress without sighting an eagle means all you saw was a couple ospreys swooping down on a fish, or two. Small deer drop down the steep hill and can often be seen on the north side of the lake.

      Watching the eagles and ospreys has actually helped my game. Aside from the display of such a large predator bird swooping down for the kill and making all the ruckus and splashing accompanied by such an event, those birds help me locate fish feeding on the surface. My reasoning is, if there was one fish on the surface there might be another. To my great surprise, this method works quite well. It might seem like foolishness, but when I see a large bird kill a surface fish, I begin rowing that direction with my fly. It might be coincidence- who can tell- but I often get a good hook up where an osprey or an eagle just scored a good snack.

Betsi and I put in with the Kayaks about two in the afternoon. It was too sunny for flies, I know, but I love bucking those odds. Truth is- there is no such thing as too sunny a day for an artificial fly! I have just proved that old myth untrue too many times to let the sunshine bother me. How about high noon and eighty-five degrees? Done that successfully. How about in twelve inches of water? Done that. The lesson I have learned is two fold. If a fish sees a fly, and it looks right to that fish, it's lunch time for the fish. The second lesson is that the proper time to go fishing is when you *want* to go fishing. Gone are the days when the light and time of day have to be just correct. Go fishing when it works for you. You will be delighted with the results.

Besti and I often put in at two in the afternoon. What with having a relaxing morning, packing the car, and hooking the kayaks on top, it is nearly always pushing lunch time by the time we leave the ranch. Then, of course, it's lunch time. After lunch we drive up to a lake, and, presto, it's two in the afternoon. In the Pacific Northwest, that's a pretty decent time to hit a lake- the morning chill is long gone, and the early risers are getting tired and going home about that time, so it works out just right. One really important aspect of getting a late start is that I don't feel quite so guilty when I load the kayak with a couple beers, if it's two in the afternoon. At first light, who could do that without a tinge of guilt?

I pushed Betsi's kayak out onto the water so she could get into the boat with her feet dry. Then I waded in with my kayak, plopped it down, and pushed off. I remember stopping a tad short to let out some fly line. My stopping irritated a young man on the bank, and he cast nearly over my kayak, but I just figured he was another one of those perpetual twelve-year olds and I was out of his reach with a touch of the oars.

It looked like a #12 Royal Coachman day, kind of like yesterday, and the day before. The truth is, I find that I am rather fixed in my ways. Most nearly all days, a Royal Coachman works just fine, so why launch out experimenting. I use what works. It's not that I never try anything else, I'm not hard nosed about the matter, it's just that fish appreciate these old flies. They are used to 'em. Royals are considered an old fashioned fly, I know. That's fair enough. Most fish are old fashioned types and we old codgers tend towards remembering the good ol' days, and in those good old days, dad used a Royal Coachman, so I use a Royal Coachman. Simple, isn't it. Sometimes, however, there are days when a #12 Royal Coachman just won't get the job done; there are days when it seems I just cannot catch a fish on a #12 Royal Coachman, so I tie on a #9.

The reason I stick with Royals is probably just psychological. After trailing around a Blue Dunn for a half an hour with no success, I usually tell myself that if I had been drowning a Royal Coachman I would have caught a fish or two. With that kind of reasoning, it is difficult for me to feel comfortable fishing other dry flies.

I don't usually fish anything but a dry fly, except that when I tie one of my own Royal Coachman on a number nine hook, I can't seem to keep it up on the surface. It just naturally sinks a couple inches below, but as soon as I start rowing, I am still able to follow the fly by its wake in the surface film, and there are few more exciting moments in fly fishing than watching the small wake from a hand-tied fly at the moment when a larger wake suddenly shows up trailing it. That is a thrill! And all wakes from a trailing trout are not the same. Some are simple little hashes through the water, but when the water rolls off the shoulders of a monster, it can make my hands start to shake.

Kress has some monster trout. Some are holdovers, but others are large brood stock that the state has decided to rid themselves of. The state dumps those large fish in Kress because the lake is, as I said, close to I-5 with great access and a boat launch their truck can back down. And dump large fish they do; some are in the five and six pound class. Occasionally, they will plant a few left over steelhead. I'm not sure what the reasoning is behind this, but the fishermen sure love it.

Right out of the box, I paralleled the southern shore. About a third of the way down the length of the lake is where most hook ups come, so I was on high alert when the fish hit. Still, the strike was pretty vicious and the pole pulled off my lap and tried to escape. I grabbed it, but was a little slow, and the fish jumped to throw the hook. It was a good looking rainbow, and looked to be about eleven inches, corkscrewing through the air and tumbling like it had never been hooked before. For some vague reason, many fish have a definite dislike to a hook in their lip.

On examining the fly, the four pound mono looked good, so I threw the same fly out on the water, again. I kept the rod in my hand and let the wind drift me for a few minutes, but it was tending to push me to the center of the lake, so I clamped my knees over the reel and took up the paddle, again. On the east end, near the lily pads and reeds, a smaller fish took the Royal Coachman. He fought well, and I let him run and jump. It's always a thrill to bring the first fish of the day to the net, and I took my time savoring the moments. In the net, the hook plopped out all on its own, so I held the rainbow up for a second to show Betsi and then lowered him back into the water.

Releasing a fish into the water always, always, makes me remember Al Gore in Alaska. I never thought I would ever write about Al Gore in a fishing story, but the memory of him in Alaska always make me smile. Here the poor guy was releasing a recovered seal lion back into the wild when things went a tad bit awry. It seams that a sea lion had been nursed back to health after being trapped and injured in a fishermen's net. The lion was doctored, fed, and housed for three months. It was nursed back to health by people who did their absolute best to help a poor, injured animal. And then they turned that animal over to Al Gore. Now, Al and his people thought it would be a great photo op, so they invited the press- who duly photographed the release back into the wild.

Al stood on the fantail of a yacht in Alaskan water with his hand on the release leaver of a stainless steal cage holding the hapless, rescued sea lion. Al mumbled something about a small step for man, or something or other, and opened the cage. Instantly, the sea lion rolled out of that cage and entered the water in that slipperier-than-oil way that only a sea lion has….., and was instantly swallowed whole by a great white shark! One minute the film footage was destined for the six o'clock news. The next second, Al was begging for the film to be destroyed. It was a priceless moment in kindness to animals.

There are no great white sharks in the waters where I fish. But there are eagles, and they are tenacious. I have had them hit fish within scant feet of my kayak. In Goose Lake, Betsi and I watched an eagle hit a German brown trout from on high. The splash was pretty tremendous, and when the spray and splash cleared, we could see the eagle sitting in the water holding a huge fish. The brown was too heavy for the eagle to fly, so he kept hold of that fish and started using his wings as paddles. It was truly an amazing sight, that great bald eagle paddling itself over to shallow water. Finally, he made it to the bank and walked up out of the lake holding a giant brown that must have measured sixteen inches, twenty if I had caught it.

In Kress Lake, I watched as the small rainbow swam away. He was legal, and I could have kept him, but it makes Betsi smile just a bit deeper if I watch them swim off. Neither of us really enjoy eating fish all that much, so the sacrifice was nothing to brag about. Sometimes, though, when I get to missing dad, and mom, and the family, and being twelve years old, I long for the taste of a small rainbow fried in an open pan with butter and some bread crumbs. Now, that's a memory for kings.

Cooking up small rainbow trout? There's a memory.

We walked up the Hamma Hamma road one August- all us us- Harold and Tommy and Johnny and Wesley and little Lenny carrying a fishing pole. It was part of my body. If we were in the woods, I had a fishing pole. The walk was longer than dad had remembered, or it was longer with five dawdling little boys than dad could imagine it would have been. I remember his frustration, during the hike, but I also remember that it was a pretty glorious hike. The road was closed, and we had it entirely to ourselves. The Olympic mountains are a splendidly beautiful and picturesque set of mountains- mostly wild and much of them are rugged to the extreme. Never has a road crossed them, so they remain pristine and unspoiled, for the most part. I was in heaven with a sharp drop off on one side open to panoramic views of the Olympics and their complex ridge upon ridge of mountains so vast that they disappear into the distance. The Olympics are thirty miles west of Seattle but are, in nature, more as if they are in Alaska. If you like it unspoiled, you will love the Olympics. But take all you need, because there are no stores and little help when you need it.

Years later, my squadron lost a Marine helicopter in the Olympics. It was a big helicopter with eleven men on board, if I remember correctly. We searched and searched, but we never found a piece of that bird. Still, nearly fifty years later, no one has come across the wreckage. In some deep and dark canyon where only falling leaves ever muster, lie the remains of some pretty good men in a hunk of green aluminum and metal engine parts. After all this time, surely they will never be found to any but the almighty.

As I remember it that August with dad and mom on the Hamma Hamma road, it was a long hike, long and thirsty. Memories are funny things. I checked it on a map, the other day, and it could not have been more than three miles from the gate across the road to the little creek where we finally gave up and sprawled down for a rest. To a bunch of little boys, it was a pretty big hike.

Mom was funny. She looked at me and simply said, "Lenny, I'm going to build a fire. You catch some fish." Wasn't that wonderful. She didn't ask me if I thought I *could* catch us something to eat. She just announced her confidence in me and started rubbing two sticks together. I was impressed with her confidence.

A little rainbow hit on the first cast behind a rock- in some impossibly fast water. No fish could live in water that fast, water that just dropped like a rock down a very steep hill towards the Hamma Hamma River. But rainbow trout are like that. They love fast, clear water. While I caught fish that had never seen a red egg on a hook, dad began cutting green twigs on which to fry the fish.

Talk about a feast! How could fish fried over an open fire with no salt and no other condiments or bread crumbs taste so fine? It was a memory many of us have taken to our graves. And so will the rest of that little band. It was a fun day, and mom made me feel like a king!

    Betsi and I rowed around Kress for a while with no action, at all, on my Coachman. We watched a bald eagle cruising high and then marveled when two ospreys swooped out of a tree and began circling for altitude. When they finally reached the eagle, they began diving on him until he gave up and flew off to the south with them fast on his heels. The next time, the eagle will chase off the ospreys.

    On the north side of the lake, I had a small tug and then nothing. I waited, but nothing happened, so I turned around and covered the water again where the fish had struck, and on the second pass, a ten inch rainbow came to the fly. It wasn't the vicious cut and slash of a cutthroat but a good solid pull, nonetheless. He ran good, actually taking line off the reel, but where could he go? In a few minutes I had him to the net and let Betsi slide her hand under his belly and lift him from the net. She giggled like a little girl, and I just laughed along with her. That fish was probably laughing, too, because I am sure that was the first time he had ever been brought to the net and then released. He was probably thinking that getting caught wasn't so bad.., and the girl was cute.

    I took a couple more fish, and then we began rowing for the launch talking about where we would like to eat. That's important, because if a fishing and kayaking excursion isn't fun for Betsi, it won't be fun for either of us, and I enjoy making her happy and having fun with her. It would be quite a different experience if she was not enjoying herself. So, I try to treat her to a fun little time out for dinner, if I can.

At the launch, I was still trailing the #12 Royal Coachman. Just as the boat was about to scrape the gravel, I noticed a super large wake behind the fly. It looked like a submarine was surfacing. That was a large fish. It made my hands shake.

That fish simply inhaled, and the fly disappeared under the surface. My fist instinct was to set the hook, but I had been there before. I waited. Sometimes, I think a fish will only partially suck a fly in, roll it around on its lips and spit it out if the fish feels anything amiss. I have lost countless fish by setting the hook just because it was in a fish's mouth but not deep enough to catch the lip. I waited. My heart was in my throat. My hands continued shaking. No tug on the line. No pull of the mono. I waited. When it came it was subtle, as if the fish might have felt the barest tip of the hook and was trying to extricate himself. I almost fell over backwards setting that hook.

I knew it was a big fish. When it jumped, everyone on the shore knew it was a big fish.., so, it jumped again. People sat their poles down and crowded around the kayak. When the fish took line out, those not already crowded around the kayak sat down their lunches. This was a big fish. It reminded me of salmon fishing in Puget Sound- when fish would pull the boat! The Kayak began pulling away from shore, and soon I had left that crowd behind. With just the correct amount of thumb pressure, I wasn't loosing any more line- but the fish was pulling the boat. No fish could do that for long. Soon, he stopped and made a fast run for the boat, again reminding me of a Puget Sound salmon. I reeled like crazy, but could not keep with his mad dash for freedom. When I gained enough line to tighten up again.., he was gone.

That's all I know about that fish. His back was dark blue like a submarine, and he could pull a kayak half way across Kress Lake. I hope he's still there, because I'm going back again in a couple days. There is absolutely no chance of hooking him, again, but you know a man just has to try. Give me a call, and we will go together if Betsi wants to stay home for an afternoon. We'll have fun.

If you have a boat.., well, the whole world of fishing changes when you have a boat- any boat.

Fishing as Good as The Good Old Days

The biggest browns are twenty-four inches, but most are ten to fourteen. No matter the size, they all strike ferociously and fight like small steelhead on light gear, and while the fishing was not as good, today, as it was years ago, it's still pretty darn good. You should have seen it twenty years ago, they say; in the good-old days, it was really really really something big. That's what is always said.

What if there was a lake with fishing as good as it was twenty years ago? Or at least as good as our *perception* of the great fishing of yesteryear?

I have found a lake where to consistently hook about twenty-five browns and manage to land ten- every single day, is the norm. With only fishing a few hours in the middle of the day? Where only an average of ten fish out of twenty or thirty, come to the net- because they are too darn mean to bring in? I think that is pretty near heaven. How good can a man want it?

The fish that get away, only achieve their freedom by being too large and mean and throw the hook, or because they jump three feet out of the water and throw the hook, or because of some foolish mistake on my part, and they throw the hook. I mean, the fish in this lake are wild and mean- just like a man wants them.

Wish I had been on that lake twenty years earlier! Twenty years ago, according to the locals, the fishing was really good! Well, I couldn't take much better. It'd be like being in heaven and they served beer.., for free.., in milk jugs.

Our favorite lake is in the Gifford Pinchot National Forest, and that is about all the hint I'm going to give; as to the name of the lake, or where the lake is located I just won't say- because I continue to fish that lake every chance I get, and I don't get that many chances to fish it, and because when I do go out on my boat in that lake, I want the fishing to still be great, like it was today, like it was twenty years ago. I won't tell you where it is, but I'll take you there. Give me a call.

It's a great lake, and Betsi and I went there last week.

As soon as the boat freed the launch, I fed out a #5 floating line with the home-made #9 Royal Coachman modified. Modified means that I couldn't really get the hang of the smaller #12 Royal Coachman, so I tied something like it, something a fly tier would scoff at, but the fish love. I inspected the fly, before throwing it out, and noted that I forgotten the last step in the building process- so it was more of a modified modified. Just a touch of glue would have sealed the hackles a little tighter, but there was no hope for it once on the water. Authentic Coachmen are supposed to float high on the surface, but I just can't get that correct, and mine ride a mite under the surface film. It's probably the weight of the #9 hook that pulls the fly under. At first, it bothered me that my home-made flies would not stay up high and dry. Then I realized that it is not so bad to have the fly sink an inch, or so, beneath the surface film, because most of the fish I have seen are not on top of the water but underneath. The majority of fish I have ever hooked have been *in* the water. Not all, but most. Well.., come to think of it- all the fish I have hooked have been in the water.., to start with. Once I hooked a flying seagull way up above the water, and last week a goose flew into my cast on the Willamette, but most fish swim below the surface of the water and fishermen are lucky that a small percentage of them look up to where our floating flies bob on, or near, the surface.

      The fish, in this particular lake, don't quite stay in the water *after* they feel the barb. Just the feel of a hook and these browns are air born. But as spectacular at aeronautical leaps as they are, those fish that refuse to jump are mostly the biguns. What those non-jumpers fail to show in acrobatic skills, they more than make up for in brawn, and this lake grows big trout. Then it grows them bigger, so when a fish doesn't jump, I start paying attention.

      Big fish are strange fish. We who go down to the sea in boats and ply the depths, still believe that bigger is better. It is probably a flaw in our genetic makeup, but I think it also comes from the way we are brought up. Would you like this supersized? New, larger packages! Bigger's better! Oh, Johnny, you are getting so big. It was *this* big, so big that it would not fit in the creel. I bought a new truck: it's eleven feet high.

     We deny our love for large, of course, but seeking the biguns keeps even the purists, among us, interested. Of course, big fish are relative. On most Olympic Peninsula rivers, a really big rainbow might be twelve inches- ten inches, if the truth be told. You catch a twelve inch rainbow, in the Olympics where I grew up, and somebody is going to paint it on canvas. I can remember being perfectly satisfied with a basket-weave creel full of eight inchers that measured nine to ten inches, every one, in the telling. But out on the Sound, I remember that a twenty pound king salmon had the inglorious nickname of "shaker". In northern California, an eight-pound winter steelhead might be a respectable fish, but in northern Oregon that fish would be looked at as merely a good start. In Alaska? You only caught *one* steelhead? And it was a little twelve pounder?

     In my mystery lake in Gifford Pinchot, a two foot long brown is a monster, and, in reality, a two-foot long fish, anywhere, is a monster fish; in a small, high-mountain lake along the Columbia River, it is especially enormous, because it is simply not possible, it is unheard of. Could a man ask for more than impossible fish? In the average northwest lake, a man might be satisfied with the normal, run-of-the-mill cutthroat of six to eight inches in length, with the dream of one fish, every great once in a while, at a foot. I know that on most lakes I am certainly satisfied with such prospects, and if you think more haughty than that, you must be from Alaska. But a fishermen's hopes are often too much, too high, and too lofty- they are simply not based in reality…

almost... and that's what keeps us going.

The dream of consistent big fish is, however, a reality for me only because of the tremendous fishing I have discovered in my secret lake. Anywhere else, within a couple hours of Portland, and most fishermen hope for a twelve incher and settle for those few eights and a ten. But, then, they are not on my mystery lake.

I played out the line way too early and close to the launch, even before I reached the prime fishable water.., but, hey, you never know! True, I have never hooked a respectable fish near the boat launch, and the non-respectables only slow me down in my hurry to get to the good water, but I'm addicted to this sport. Did I mention that? After a few minutes, though, I approached water where one needs to slow down, and regroup, and to start paying attention.

It probably is not necessary to row, except for the obvious need to keep the line tight. It's a fly, out there, not a lure. Even real, authentic dead flies sit still on water, but I reason, to myself, that if I row very very slowly, I will cover more fish, whatever that means.

Perhaps it can be compared to bowling. It's not, really like bowling, because bowling balls don't swim, but if you just placed your ball on the arrows and waited for the pins to come and knock themselves unconscious on the ball, you would be nuts. But what if *some* of the pins could go looking for the ball? Then why would you want to throw it down the alley? Because the ball would then roll down the alley *and* be chased by the pins that could swim. That way, you would get double exposure.

Some fish, in a lake, stay put in one place, while others *swim* around. So, they are like bowling pins that can maneuver on their own always looking around for a ball to hit. For the dear reader educated in public schools, this example is a metaphor- or a simile- I'm not sure, for I was educated in public schools. If I just let that fly sit there on top of the water, only a few fish will see it, but if I row around I cover both stationary fish and moving fish.

Being sedentary is getting easier now that I'm edging into my twilight years where girls look past me to some twelve-year old with an eleven foot-high truck, and where high-heeled waitresses call me sir. Last year three high school kids came to my house to interview me about ancient history in Vietnam. Like, "What was the civil war like, grandpa?" It is true that while I am trying to learn to relax and just hang around- and fish slower and more meaningfully- sedentary remains difficult for me. So bowling pins, or no, the real reason I row, instead of sit in one spot- is that I just can't *do* that. I couldn't do that in police work. I can't do that elk and deer hunting, and I can't do that fishing. Some people can sit still for hours. It kills me.

I try to relax into the peaceful and tranquil sport of kings, this fishing of idyllic waters. I tell myself to put the oar down, sit there in the kayak, and watch the fly look authentic. Don't move. Leave it alone. I can't. I want to, but I just can't. Look, if fish swim, *and* I row around, it's like throwing the bowling ball down the alley *and* having the pins swimming around looking for the ball! It's like a multiplication of effort, or something complicated, like that.

Plus, the take of a fish is more apt to result in a solid hookup when I am rowing, and if I row, that fly will be scanned by a lot more fish than sitting still (Maybe. Who really knows?) While rowing, if I throw out a five weight line on a light rod and reel, and one of those giant cuts hit my fly on the run, I have learned to have that rod clamped tight between my knees- or go a-grabbing at it while it skitters away.

I remember hooking cutts, on my native Olympic Peninsula. Dad would point out the red slash under the chin. "That's how you know it's a cut," he would say. I don't remember anything definitive in the play of an Olympic Peninsula cutthroat that would distinguish it from a rainbow. But in this lake in the Gifford Pinchot National Forest, there are German brown trout, and those browns are vicious! They don't gently inhale a little fly off the surface- that want to devour it. On examination, their jaws seem a little larger than cutthroat I have taken, and the browns will have a series of three or four red spots along their dorsal line. These browns are game. They *want* to strike. And they want to kill whatever it is they are chasing. While a rainbow will gently nibble on a worm; these browns want to obliterate their target, they want to annihilate it and consume it. I love these fish! Remember the reason that Alligator Dundee could not afford to miss when he threw a rock? He was hungry. With these German brown trout, it's like the take, and the run, are one and the same thing, and an angler had better hold on to that pole, because when these fish throw a rock- they are hungry.

So, I row. Very slowly, but I row.

I pulled that fly through the water as if it was something homemade in which I could take great pride. It was. My oversize coachman always create a small riffle on the surface of the water, so I mostly always know where the fly is sliding through the top film. Often I can see, behind that riffle, off to the left or right, a dark, smooth section of water appear. Then a fin. And wham; a feather I found on the ground, and a few hairs from my last elk, and some red thread I stole from Betsi's sewing basket fooled a wild high-lakes German brown trout into thinking it was something delicious.

My favorite take, from one of these brown trout, is a snatch and grab aeronautical feat that always brings a laugh and a lunge for the pole. One second, the fly can be tracking smoothly and quietly- when from several feet below, a fish breaks the surface and is two feet in the air with my elk-hair-on-a-hook before the fish even knows the fly is biting back. These fish aren't like bowlers. Most fish don't *learn* how to fight on a fly line. It's a one-time-only experience for most fish, and they get an itty bit excited at the bite of the hook. For some reason, I don't think these crazy browns enjoy the hook all that much, for they go nearly as berserk on the take... as I do.

On those rare occasions when I see many fish feeding on the surface I will rarely, but sometimes, park the boat in the shallows and watch for a surface rise from a hungry trout. At those times, it's instantly cover the rise with the Coachman, or just plain miss the opportunity. In the shallows near the reeds is where the big ones feed openly on the surface, and if they splash taking a bug, they will often take a second bug from the same, exact, spot if my cast is quick and accurate. I love that. Whoosh! Splash! Bug Gone. Then I have time for one quick back cast followed by spot-on accuracy laying that fly right on the arrows, and if I'm lucky- Whammo! That fish thought two was better than one. It's a strike.

Of course, the trouble with big fish, in shallow water, is that there are few places for an excited fish to go. The water is too shallow for the fish to run deep. The hook hurts; so they don't want to run away from the boat. So they jump! They jump clean out of the water; they shake their heads, and it's on that first violent and thrashing jump where a fish often tosses the hook. I don't care. I just laugh and laugh. To touch a two foot German brown trout, for even an instant, I am a fortunate man. Fishing is not the sport of those who happen to be kings. It is the sport of fishing that makes the man a king!

Very occasionally, there is a different kind of take. It's a gentle thing, but I have learned to be wary of it. It is like a soft kiss on your cheek.., from my third grade teacher. Miss Clarabel Johnson kept a wooden ruler behind her back. She would smile soo sweetly, and then- whammo! Sometimes, a brown's tug is just a gentle gulp and a soft tug on the line. There may, or may not be, the faintest soft ripple of water at the gulp. I have learned not to set the hook on this kind of a take, but to gently lift the rod and let the line tighten on its own accord... because, brother, that's a big fish with a wooden ruler behind his back.

I won't tell you where this mystery lake is. I quit telling. But I'll go there with you, if you are a nobody, like me, and have an eleven foot tall truck and are over twelve years old. It helps, of course, if you know how to bowl.

The biggest browns are twenty-four inches, but most are ten to fourteen. No matter the size, they all strike ferociously and fight like small steelhead on light gear, and while the fishing was not as good, today, as it was years ago, it's still pretty darn good.

It was the Best of Times

If I remember correctly, I was only about eight or nine when dad took mom and us three boys for a trip to the Strait of Jaun de Fuca. As every school boy knows, those who have the benefit of a public school education, that large body of water was named for the Spanish explorer Strait- Juan de Fuca Strait. The Strait meets the Pacific Ocean at Forks, Washington, and runs about ninety-five miles east to Port Angeles. If it were not for the Strait of Juan de Fuca, Port Angeles would be a bedroom community of Victoria, B.C. But there it is; God put a fifteen mile barrier between Canada and the United States, because the Almighty knows that good fences make good neighbors.

Just in the last few years, for some strange reason, the Strait may have been renamed the Sallis Sea. I couldn't really make heads or tales out of the myriads of commissions studying the issue, so I'm not sure if it has happened already or those politicians, we pay so highly, are just fixin' to rename something that is not theirs to rename.

The name Sallis was created by some hyper concerned marine biologist who wanted to make the world more aware of the northwest waterways between the Pacific Ocean and Seattle - all this to ostensibly create concern over the environment and to strengthen the much aligned ecosystem.

    Only time will tell if the name catches on or if it slips away to the dust bins of higher learning. If they wanted to change the name, they could have at least stolen an Indian name. There are enough Indian names in the Pacific Northwest that they could have used one of them- Makah, Skokomish, Quinault, Hoh, Elwa Klallam, Squaxin. There are so many Indian names that I'm sure one tribe or another wouldn't miss a really good one. I vote to rename all the waterways from the Pacific Ocean to the end of Puget Sound simply Salt Chuck. Salt Chuck means- here it is- wait for it- *salt water*- or in the ancient vernacular of the Snohomish Indians- klatuu barada nikto.

    Changing the name of all the salt waters of the northwest to Sallis sounds rather suspicious to me, and I heard a rumor, some place, that Sallis is the maiden name of that now famous marine biologist's wife- in which case I could understand it if Sallis meant something like- little cute thing in the morning- or dove of my heart- something choice, like that. But what that body of water is- is an enormous fat piece of water in which you could drown Montana, so if this wonderful marine biologist's wife has a backside as large as the big sky country, the name change makes sense. Otherwise, leave it alone.

    Dad threw us in the Oldsmobile, and we took out of Bremerton by Kitsap Way and then through Belfair where we stopped for gas that was priced seventeen cents a gallon. Then he purchased twelve hamburgers for a dollar from the Crazy Eric drive in.

God bless Crazy Eric for that! Twelve for a dollar! I just cannot think of anything to compare it to, in today's world, where twelve burgers would cost pretty near a hundred dollars and so does a tank full of gas.

We took the South Shore Road and stopped for a minute at Belfair State Park. After a look at the spectacular vistas and a walk on the beach, we continued on and our spirits rose as we rounded the corner of Hood Canal to drive through the Skokomish Indian Reservation. Then we headed north along highway 101 toward Sequim and Daboob Bay. All good names of places I wish I was headed towards tomorrow. It used to take all day to get to Point Angeles from Bremerton via Hamma Hamma and Oyster Bay. The speed limit was twenty-five for a good portion of the trip due to the squirrelly roads along Hood Canal, for the Olympic Mountains are a pretty rugged set of hills, and they just slam down hard against what would someday be named the Sallis Sea. For most of the trip, there is enough shoreline for a two way road, two houses and… a steep drop into the salt chuck. It's roadway, two feet of gravel, and oysters for about a hundred miles. Hitch hikers have to hold their thumbs close up against their chests. There is a roadway sign just outside Dosewallips State Park that simply reads, "Naro Rd".

When we finally arrived in Port Angeles, we were all dead tired, exhausted and still had many miles to go to our destination at the Sol Duc Hot Springs. Dad was never a stickler for details, so just outside of Port Angeles, he pulled off the road and under a likely looking little bridge where we could all throw out our sleeping bags. He didn't have to encourage us much. I remember being asleep taking off my shoes.

This is one of my special memories. My memory is heightened, I suppose, because it was really not much of a pull out, not much of a little creek under the bridge, and not much a camping spot, but there I was, in my boyhood, with dad and mom and my two older brothers- in the golden, good old days- and the memory was heightened because it involved me being the hero by catching fish. One way, or another, if I caught a fish somewhere- I always remember that spot.

That little creek held marvelous fat sea run cutthroat eager to take a little red egg from a little boy's little fishing pole. Those fish were crossovers; half the time, that little creek was fresh water spilling down off the Olympics, and half the time, the creek was flooded by the Strait of Juan de Fuca. The creek was only about a foot deep, perhaps two, and was clear as crystal- I could see every inch of the creek bottom, but I did not see any fish. The only break in the sea shell and sand covered bottom was a five foot log submerged lengthwise with the current.

I sprung out of bed at first light. I never could sleep past first light on fishing trips. The excitement and the anticipation of it all was too much for a little toe headed kid with an imagination. Fishing sure beat the normal day for this nine-year old.

If I held my leader and hook up to the east and squinted, I could just make out the bend in the hook and the hole to pass the leader through. From there, it was easy; a couple of grannies, and I was home free.

The pop of the lid on the little egg jar was so loud that I thought the family would awaken. I figured that Dad was probably already awake, for he was always on sentinel duty. As I had drifted off to sleep, the night before, I remember him muttering something about watching the tide, during the night, to make sure that our little family wasn't washed away. I remember him always watching out for us and taking care of us, and that is a good memory. If he was still here, and reading the things I write, he would probably tell me to get over all this hero worship stuff and get on with the fishing story, but he isn't- so I'm not about to.

Now that I'm sixty-four years of age, I am not always sure what to think of my memories of dad. If he hadn't been my dad, I think I still would have admired him. Maybe then we could have been friends. *My* children don't seem plagued with the hero worship thing, and that's okay with me. I have often told them that adults with such common backgrounds should settle for being good friends. Somehow, they can't quite manage that, but to be honest my feelings for them are not merely friendly- so all in all, I don't know what to do with my own advancing old age and children who are forty, or going bald, or have ten children of their own. It seems like I always want more, they are always satisfied with less, and so we just settle for pizza.

I wanted to fish that little creek, but when the growing light finally got around to showing it to me, I just stood there and looked at it with a mixture of dejection and disappointment. How to fish a one foot deep creek with every stone and shell on the bottom highly visible? I didn't see how that little stretch of water could hold a fish, and I couldn't fish the mouth of the creek where it finally emptied into the salt chuck because of the expanse of mud I would have to muck my way through. I was just about to give up, when my eye caught the only underwater feature in that little creek- that log lying with the current. It seemed like there just may have been a little channel carved in the bottom along the sand at the base of that log. What choice did I have? There were either fish hiding behind that log, or I could crawl back into my sleeping bag.

Dad didn't have much incentive to supply us kids with expensive reels or rods. I can understand that. We were just kids. In a boat in Puget Sound, he used to tie his fishing rods down so we wouldn't drop them over the sides. (He didn't tie us- just the fishing rods. There's a moral, there, somewhere.) Somehow, I acquired some cheap little reel with plastic mother of pearl handles. It was impossible to cast with, so I just figured out a way. By pulling the line out and spooling it at my feet, I could then cast a weighted line out ten or twelve feet. Actually, it made for pretty accurate, spot-on distance casts, because once the correct length of line was at my feet, all I had to do was haul off and heave it a good one. The line would always go the exact distance desired. So, once I had that log dialed in, casting to just my side of it was easy. I put on one of those ultra-cheap red and white bobbers about twelve inches above my split shot and cast away. It was, as I recall it, the perfect drift. How could it be otherwise? The bobber settled just upriver from the log and drifted straight down current along the length of that little log, and when the bobber passed the end of the log, it was pulled under water by some strange and mystical force.

Whammo! A very healthy eleven inch cutthroat had been hiding behind the tail end of that log just watching for healthy looking tidbits floating down the river. It seems that the log was a natural funnel for anything edible. Bugs, flies, and whatever gross things trout eat would float down that little creek, bump up against that log and tumble down current towards the Strait. For years that cutthroat had settled behind the tail end of that log and feasted on goodies floating by.

And that first fish had friends.

I put them on a stick.

When, finally, dad and mom awoke, I had a stringer of large and heavy cutthroat ready for breakfast. Dad tumbled out of his bag first and made his way up to me rubbing his beard and hair. He looked like he was still asleep. I laughed because he looked like a bear that had just tumbled out of a hole in the ground. "Uh?" he managed. "Had any luck?" It was as if he had managed to create a monster with a fishing pole and had some responsibility to at least appear interested.

All I said was, "Couple."

"Uh," he repeated and stumbled off.

Mom finally, after about two years, came over and obligingly asked how I was doing. Silently, I held up half a dozen pretty impressive sea-run cutthroat trout. She shrieked and hurried off to start a fire for breakfast, and dad broke out in a large grin when he saw me proudly hold up the stringer. "Got to teach you to throw a fly," he called from his bedroll.

There wasn't anymore fishing to be done what with cooking breakfast and packing up the car, so I put my rod away and jumped on Harold and Tom who were acting as if they were still sleeping.

As the old green Oldsmobile bounced up onto the highway and passed over the bridge, I strained high in my seat to get one last look at that little creek and the log running with the current. *I will be back to visit you again. I promise!*

So, I did.

But by my calculations, it was forty-two years. There was a small, ratty looking house built right over the turnout where dad had pulled the Oldsmobile. I guess I have seen more trash spread all over a front yard, but I don't remember where that might have been. And the healthy, fat, sea-run cutthroat hiding behind that little log lying with the current, in that little creek off the Strait of Juan de Fuca? God only knows. Hope so.

Just outside of Port Angeles, dad pulled off the road and under a likely looking little bridge where we could all throw out our sleeping bags. Glad he did.

Lower Lena Lake

For a brief span of time, I was in the Boy Scouts. It was kind of like being in the Marines, without the explosives, and we all got to go home at night- which is what each and every Marine desires most of all regardless of how big and tough they all put on. What really made it worth it all, was that the Boy Scouts took me fishing every once in a while.

On one trip, we hiked up to Lower Lena Lake, off the Hamma Hamma River Road. That's a once in a lifetime hike and camping experience, except that if you live in the area, like I did as a young man, you could do it every weekend- which is what I was always begging for.

I remember my fellow scouts being all complaints and whimperings as we hiked the three miles up to the lake. It was a pretty tough hike, and for those boys who never did anything but watch their televisions, they found the hike murder. Admittedly, it is straight up the side of a mountain for a few miles, but for some strange reason those complaining boys grew up and took their children on that same, grueling hike. Life is funny, like that.

Lower Lena can be a fantastic day hike, in and

out in a few hours, or you can camp along the lake and enjoy some pretty incredible scenery. Rocks as high as castles line the lake, and a fair size little river tumbles into the lake on the northeast corner. The camping sites are numerous with glorious views of the lake. It's a deep lake, so a fishermen needs a rubber boat or settle for just plunking from the shoreline.

Once again, I held my line up to the first light of the morning and strained to make out that little hole in the hook for the leader to pass through. No one else was even thinking of squirming in their sleeping bags. I couldn't figure that out? Those kids could sleep at home every night but are only on Lower Lena once in a great while. I was so filled with excitement, that my legs were bouncing up and down making the threading of the line even more difficult.

Our troop had camped in a lovely campsite at the mouth of the creek. From my sleeping bag, the lake was spread out before me like the sea of crystal in Revelations, with gray granite stones that must have been twenty feet high along the shore. It was really a tremendous sight. Here and there, the rise from a fish could be seen. I could hardly wait. I have always been like that. Just before fishing, I am still like a kid on Christmas morning. To me, it is one of the most exciting times. Who knows what opportunities await, what lies, there, under the dark, mysterious surface of a bright, new morn?

The line rigged, I climbed out onto the logjam at the mouth of the creek, but cast after cast, no fish rose from the likely looking rocky bottom. I threw pale orange salmon eggs until my arm began to pain.

Nothing. Zipp. So, I tried just dropping the egg at my feet and letting it ride the current along the length of the log on which I was standing. Vacant. Nobody home.

I marveled at the lake, at the scenic creek, at the trees, a couple eagles in the background gaining altitude and climbing into the heavens. I marveled at no fish. Could the creek simply be fished out with all the crowds of tourists coming and going? I scratched my head. I guess that was possible, but I reminded myself that most people don't really know how to fish. Where, then, were the fish this morning?

The pale orange and golden colored salmon eggs were a step up from the harder, bright red colored eggs that were prevalent with many novice fishermen. Usually, I sneered at those who would throw such sick looking bait. But, I reasoned, my more expensive eggs were a no show- and I only had two kinds of eggs to try. The first cast with one single, little, smelly, brightly stained red salmon egg- a huge cutthroat slid out from under my log and nailed the egg like it was something special! That was great fun! I tightened up the drag and was able to keep the fish from running and glad of it, for if that fish had taken off and made a run for the lake, there was no way to follow- the log jam just made that impossible. So, I solved the problem of the fish running into the lake, but not how to take possession of my prize.

When the fish tired, I was faced with an intriguing problem; the log I was fishing from was quite large- large enough that it barely moved when a small boy stood on it. It was round. It was no problem to walk carefully along its length, and it was no problem to balance myself on top, but how to reach the water to bring in a fish? I had no net, for I rarely needed a net for pan sized cutthroat and rainbows. But I sure needed one, then. Every time I reached for that tired out fish, I would start to loose my balance. Toppling into an ice cold, high mountain creek at first light of morning was not a fun proposition. The fish was there. I was there. How to twain it up? I knew that at any second, the fish might regain enough strength to mount one more impressive run- and who knows? It might try for the security of deep water out in the lake, and I had to get that fish, and I had to latch onto it now.

Faced with desperation, I simply resorted to the simplest method I could devise. I pulled the cutthroat up onto the log and jumped on it. The move was not pretty. It lacked finesse. Nothing squirms like a fresh caught rainbow trout or cutthroat suddenly pulled out of the water, but my advanced technique of pouncing worked just fine.

So, I did it again.

It is my guess that fish do not learn by example any better than men. Every cutt under that log watched as the one before it darted out from under the log and took a shiny, red salmon egg, never to return. Every one of them that darted out after that red salmon egg ended up being dragged up onto the dry part of that log they had all spent their life hiding under. Six in all, and it was great fun in the doing.

Boy, was there a hero in camp when I walked into camp in front of dozens of Boy Scouts. I was carrying six of the brightest, healthiest cutthroat any of them had ever seen! I was regaled with offers of friendship, hailed as somebody very special, palm branches were thrown in my path.

We scouts were leaving right after lunch, so I cleaned those fish and threw them in my backpack to take home to the family.

From the kitchen sink, dad picked up one of the fish and examined it. His expression was of appreciation coupled with some vague look I could not read. His eyes got kind of dreamy, for a second, and then he remarked that he remembered the fishing being pretty healthy at the mouth of the creek- when he was a boy- and that was a couple summers before! Why he hadn't returned, he had no idea? After a few seconds, dad placed the trout back with the others and took to his chair, and sat there watching TV for about an hour without saying a word. The set was turned off, but I don't think he noticed.

In the kitchen, mom and I were readying the fish for dinner, when I told her how disturbed dad had become. She left the fish to me and went to stand in the living room door. After a minute, dad turned and smiled at her. "He's a good kid, huh?"

"Well, yeah."

Jefferson Lake

Jefferson Lake is one of those lost lakes. I don't quite remember where it is, but it seems to be somewhere up around the Hamma Hamma. It is a small, high mountain lake open only in the summers when the road clears. Its waters are deep and cold, and it is picturesque. The only down side to Jefferson is that there are not too many good camping spots on the lake. Our family went there, mainly, because there was really only one camping site on the lake, and if we got it first- we would not be bothered by other campers having noisy parties and disturbing our family solitude.

The camping site was terrible to get to- straight down a steep bank filled with blackberries and fallen logs. And the campsite was looked down on from the road, so there wasn't much privacy from the prying eyes of people driving by in cars. What saved the site was that there just weren't that many cars that ever drove on that road- and once in camp, the lake and surrounding mountains were absolutely beautiful.

Dad had camped there as a boy, and remembered it fondly. At that time, the lake had been filled with monster cutthroat trout. It was a fond memory for him. In the steamy jungle of the South Pacific, all dad ever wanted was to return home and marry his high school sweetheart, have a family and take them camping and fishing. He prayed that he would live through the war to be the typical all-American father. He made it, too.

The campsite at Jefferson Lake was in the bottom of a deep canyon, and the walls of the canyon framed the lake like a natural picture frame. It was quite lovely. Right in front of the campsite the little creek ran into the lake and formed a long spit of land that was just about perfect for someone with a fly pole.

We boys circled the lake as soon as we could get out of the setting up camp chores. As I remember it, there were huge, two story granite boulders all along the eastern shore. Where there were no boulders, there were deep tangles of brush. From the lofty perch on top of the boulders we made out schools of cutthroat trout patrolling the shore. I was aware that fish traveled in schools in salt water, but I was not aware that they did so in small, high mountain lakes. We put most of the fish on ten to fourteen inches with a few pretty enormous specimens mixed in! Occasionally, a lone fish would pass the school going in the opposite direction.

As soon as we saw those huge schools of fish, we boys began throwing single eggs on small hooks. As soon as those fish saw those single eggs on small hooks, they would swim around them and then continue their weird clockwise trek. We threw pale yellow salmon eggs, bright red salmon eggs, and a bright silver spoon. We threw everything we could think of until the sun burned us to a crisp and drove us to the shad of the campsite.

It was always dad's opinion that if you could see a fish in the water you might as well not try to fish for it. He said sighting a fish ruined the fun of fishing, and if we could see the fish- the fish could see us just as well. "Would you bite on a hook, if you knew someone was trying to kill you?" He made sense, but it was like an addiction. We could see hundreds of large cutthroat trout going round and round like someone had put in a quarter. It was weird.

I put a bobber on the line and threw it where I thought the next wave of fish would pass. They did. They passed right by. We should fish elsewhere, dad said at lunch the first day. But we could see hundreds of fish off those granite boulders. We knew where the fish were- we just could not get them interested.

Harold dug up two grubs, and we tried those. A fish actually swam up to a grub and.., then swam off. We cheered.., almost.

Finally at the end of the day, we dragged ourselves into camp, three boys tuckered out. Dad had been sitting in a camp chair all day watching us casting and casting to the schools of fish. He watched as we jumped in anticipation, slumped in disappointment, and then finally slinked off in dejection. What should we do, we asked him? Dad was a funny guy. He had already answered that question, so he just stared into the fire and then turned his attention to the lake. We waited for about a century and a half, for dad to answer, and then we ambled off to find adventure somewhere else.

As the sun was going down, we were all seated around the camp watching the shadows work their way down the granite boulders. Mom found some lotion for the sunburns, and dad pulled out his fly rod. I thought that looked pretty glorious and got a little excited at the prospect of watching dad casting to rising trout on that picturesque peninsula. When dad had strung the pole and put on a small black fly, he turned to us boys. "Tommy, why don't you take this fly rod out on that little spit of land and see what happens in the fading light?" He could have slain Tom with a piece of straw!

I slumped down in my camp chair, for I could certainly handle a fly rod. Harold didn't say a thing; he could never do more with a fly rod than tangle himself up in a ball of mono and dark brown floating line. Dad handed Tommy the fly rod and asked him to take it out on the spit of land that floated on the sunset of fire and brimstone water. That spit looked like a dark shadow in a pit of flame.

"Tommy," he said quietly. "You will go away to college in a few weeks, and this may be your last fishing trip with the family for quite a while." Tommy took the rod and returned dad's gaze but did not say a word. "You have been trying to catch fish all day, but it just did not work. Tonight, just enjoy the fishing. Don't worry about fish. Just enjoy the time with the rod and line."

Bats darted around Toms head as he stood on that spit of land. His feet were lost in shadow so that it looked as if he were floating in sunset and flame. How the bats stayed out of the swirling fly line, I have not a clue. I could almost feel Tom's concentration, how he kept his right arm close to his body and let the rod throw the line. After a few well timed back casts, Tom aimed a foot above the water and let the line go- it floated down onto the yellow, red, and orange surface like a cherry blossom. It was a thing of beauty.

The family watched intent on Tom's demonstration. The fly floated high and dry undisturbed on the surface film. Harold stirred the fire, and I tried to watch dad for any little sign of his approval of Tom's casting, but he looked content to just take an awful long time to fill his pipe. Mom sat rocking in her camp chair sipping quietly on her coffee.

Tom, slowly and meticulously brought the line in for another cast.

I don't remember Tommy catching any fish that evening. He was content to cast and cast- determined to justify dad choosing him to hold the treasured fly rod. It was like a holy evening. We all sat there watching quietly. Out in the sunset, Tommy made us a memory. Nice gift, that, but he always was the thoughtful one.

The next morning, after breakfast, dad asked if I would like to fish a lake nearby. I jumped at the chance, and he drove me to a small piece of water. We both stood there looking at what some people might call a lake. It was shallow. From the little launch area, it seemed as if I could see the bottom of the entire lake.

"Okay," I drawled. "I guess I could give it a try."

"You have the lunch your mother prepared?"

"Yeess."

"Good," he said. "I will come back for you in the evening."

"Ookkaay."

Dad turned to go and then turned back. "Lenny, you are only fifteen, but you know how to fish. You.., uh.., take to it, like I did. Enjoy yourself today."

I had to admit to myself that I was a little confused.

"I gave you fishing," he said. "I introduced you to it, but you have embraced it like nobody's business. Tommy is leaving for college. Harold is going into the Marines."

I am pretty sure, looking back on it now, that I might have been fairly loud in my exclamation, for I was pretty well shocked right out of my kids, at the news of Harold and the Marines.

"Harold is going into the Marines next week. Today, I am going to take him for a long walk."

"Yeah?" was all I could think to answer.

"If my memory serves me correctly," continued dad, "I hunted here once when I was a young boy. Up the road a little. I thought I might like to find that spot one more time before I.., I would like to see a particular meadow, once again.

"Harold and I have never really gotten along very well. He and I.., well.., well, we never hit it off, and I guess we never will, but I'm going to take him for a walk." Dad scratched his head and then continued. "I don't know why I am telling you this- perhaps I'm just practicing for Harold. But, well.., you know there is a war on. Some boys don't come back from that kind of thing, and there are a few things I would say to the boy. Anyway, you fish here. I will be back after Harold and I get back from our walk."

Then he laughed, and on his face spread that infectious ear to ear grin under a bent and crooked nose, the left overs from his own war years before. "You just have fun on the lake, Lenny!"

Luckily for me, I found a raft in the water. I waded out to the crickety old bunch of logs, found it seaworthy and poled out into the lake. Nowhere was the lake over three feet deep. I took off my straw cowboy hat and rubbed my face and then muttered as I unwound a night crawler from the ball of worms in my bait box. "Tommy is going off to college. Harold is going into the Marines.., and I'm stuck fishing a puddle."

It was ten in the morning. I ate my lunch.

I fished through noon without a bite from a fish and wondered if the lake was sterile. It looked more like a water dog lake than anything else. About one, in the afternoon, I gave up on fishing and just laid back in the sun. I just cast the worm thirty feet out and put the straw hat over my head, and went to sleep to the gentle rocking of the raft, the smell of the straw hat cooking away in the sun, and the dreams of the contented, for although my world was just about to be altered drastically by my two older brothers leaving, they weren't gone yet, and I was in the mountains fishing on a raft in the summertime.

When the sun finally began sinking behind the

hills and trees, and the shadows began creeping down to the shore of the lake, I poled over to the launch. Whatever happened to dad and Harold, I decided it was about time for this lad to find his way back to camp and mom's sunburn lotion. To my luck, dad pulled up just as I stepped off the raft. "I've been watching you from up on the road," he admitted. "You have an unusual technique."

I was embarrassed because I did not know he had been watching. "It worked," I offered and held up a string of cutthroat that anyone would be proud to claim. "I tried everything I knew, then I just gave up and threw out a worm and went to sleep. Left alone, those fish did all right."

Dad lifted the string of fish, hefted the load and smiled. "You know. I have a confession to make. I fished this lake, once, when I was a boy. My father brought me. I caught a tremendous string of cutthroat-just like this one. I was wondering if they had gone away?"

The fish hadn't gone away. They were still there.

Now, forty years later, I find myself desiring to find Jefferson and Elk lakes and to see if the cutthroat have gone away. Nearly everyone else in this story has.

Jefferson Lake is one of those lost lakes. I don't quite remember where it is, but it seems to be somewhere around the Hamma Hamma. It is a small, high mountain lake open only in the summers when the road clears. Its waters are deep and cold, and it is picturesque.

If you know where Jefferson and Elk lakes are, drop me a line.

If you know where mom, and dad, and Harold are…

My First Steelhead
Without a hook

And My Second Steelhead
That Wasn't Mine

It was on the Wilson. The Wilson is a strange river. It is many different things to thousands of users. In the summer, the water flow decreases and it becomes low, clear, and useless to a fisherman, but the kids love it. They float in the pools on inner tubes, jump off rocks, and swing on ropes. Teens own the Wilson in August.

Often in September, but for sure in October, the water level rises and the steelhead begin to think about the Wilson. The early fisherman, the ones who just can't wait, will start plying the empty water, and there are enough in this group that the pullouts begin filling up in rehearsal for November through February when you can't *buy* a parking spot along the river and the water is filled with large and fresh steelhead.

Down the coast of Alaska, Canada, Washington, and finally Oregon the fish came on their return trip. They manage, somehow, to make it through a gauntlet of fishermen at the mouth of

Tillamook Bay and then chose one of the four rivers that hit the bay in the town of Tillamook. Up the river of their choice, they battle over rapids and then shallows that take their breath away. They jump the falls under the Kansas Creek bridge. The hurdles are numberless. The drive to reproduce is enormous.

I suppose, it is not fair, really, that we choose that particular time to attack steelhead. They have other things on their minds. It's a little akin to rolling a drunk at closing time when that drunk is thinking more about.., well, he's really thinking an awful lot like a migrating steelhead.

On the Wilson, those eager fishermen could stay home in September, October and most of November. Tradition says that steelhead fishing begins on Thanksgiving. It might be true, for you can surely *fish* for steelhead beginning on Thanksgiving day, but good luck. Even as late into the season as Thanksgiving, it's a little early for the Wilson. Nobody told the steelhead to start up the river on Thanksgiving. Some years they do, but most years they delay their excursion until December.

The day I caught my first steelhead was a week before Christmas. Now, anyone who knows the Wilson River knows that the week before Christmas, you can catch a steelhead on a can opener. But I hadn't been able to catch a steelhead on nothing, notime, nowhow. I was a young man, and I was eager, but I didn't have any can openers. I threw out eggs. Then I threw out a spoon. Then I threw out… well, you get the picture; I tried everything in my box. I was fishing the Power Line Hole, and I had it pretty much to myself. It was a good thing I was alone, for I was embarrassing myself… to death. Finally, I walked upriver from the Power Line Hole to a series of small holes above. A search of my vest turned up nothing new, nothing I had not tried. Then, in the bottom of my right vest pocket, under a couple loose fish hooks, a few pieces of lead, a suspicious looking empty one ounce bottle, and an old cracker I pulled out a small green flatfish. That particular flatfish must have been in that pocket for years. I used to fish it for trout with my brother Tom when I was still in high school. How it got in my fishing vest, ten years later, is a mystery.

    I have never seen another bank angler fish for steelhead with a green flatfish, never before, never since. I looked at the flatfish for a second, shrugged, and tied it on. I have since learned that it is not so much what you fish with as much as that you fish it correctly. It's a little akin to that drunk looking for a red headed woman *outside* the bar. The can opener would have worked if I had fished the correct place, at the correct depth, with the correct presentation; these are things that are of paramount importance when fishing for steelhead or chasing red headed women. But I didn't know that yet. That drunk needs to go *inside* the bar. I read that somewhere. As I said, I, personally, have no knowledge of red headed women, or bars, and at the time I had scant knowledge of steelhead.

    I tied on the green, frog-patterned flatfish.

    Pretty much, everything I had thrown out, all day, had snagged, and I was beginning to believe that steelheading might be an expensive pastime. I was not surprised when right off I snagged, yet again. I was extremely frustrated and just yanked on the pole. The snag, of course, yanked back. That was interesting.

It got a lot more interesting when the snag decided to run down river from small pool to small pool, because there was so much ice that it was difficult to walk alongside the river, and impossible to follow along the shear face of several large rock outcroppings. I did though. It was my first steelhead. I found tow holds and hand holds that could not be found when I later tried to retrace my steps. It was like a miracle. That path could not be taken with rope and crampons, but I chased that fish until he stopped in a larger pool before the river flattened out. There was no water below him, and that fish knew it. It was fight, here, for freedom or die trying. It was him or me.

The fish was content to stay in the larger pool, and I was just as content to let him lie. After a while, though, he began dashing around the pool, and then after one jump and a small run, he tired fast and I brought him to the bank, but the bank was one flat rock slab tilted at an angle toward the water. Every time I got next to the water, to make a grab for the fish, I began to slide on the ice. I backed up, tried a different angle and, again, began to slide toward the water. All the time, the fish was on his side resting. All the time, I was sure that at any moment he would awake and begin to thrash wildly about. I figured that if that fish began thrashing wildly, it would be an easy thing for him to break the line and rocket back into the deeper pool and away.

Thinking back on my early steelheading, as difficult as it was to learn how to consistently hook steelhead, *landing* the fish was just as troubling. Steelhead are large fish. You can not simply lift them with a small trout net. Most any net capable of holding a steelhead is too big to carry along a river, weighs too much to pack about, and is too clumsy to work with just one hand while you try to hold the fishing rod in the other. There's the kicking method. I have watched fishermen try to work a big fish to the river and then kick the fish toward shore, but that seems to fail as often as it works. What a heartbreaker to get a big and precious fish nearly to the beach and then loose it with a kick and an Indian cuss word. Gilling fish seemed like a workable solution, but I found that in most circumstances it is not possible. These are big, heavy fish. The solution I finally settled on, and which I still use today, is to tire the fish as much as possible, reeling the fish in to about boot height in the water and suddenly sweeping the fish up and onto the bank. Usually, at the point when the head of the fish hits dry gravel, the fish starts flopping pretty wildly, but as long as I keep its head pointed towards dry land, it flops itself up and out of the water. It is not elegant. It simply gets the fish out of the water.

      My first steelhead on the Wilson just about won his freedom when I tried to bring him to land. Down on one knee, I leaned out absolutely as far out as I could and then I reached for the gill.., and my knee started slipping on the thick ice. Finally, with a last little push, I reached the gill plate, but the fish saw my move and clamped his gill plate closed tightly. Just then, at that very inoperative moment, the flatfish's hook pulled free- but the split-ring between the hook and flatfish body hung up on a bit of soft looking skin in the fish's mouth.

So, there I was- in the dead of winter, on a lonely, frozen slab of ice with my first steelhead, and the hook popped out- *and* that lucky bit of skin did not look like it would hold for long. In that little millisecond time stood still. The loose bit of skin holding the hook was tearing, and the fish was sliding backwards into the water. At that very opportunistic time, the fish's gill plate opened slightly- just as the flatfish, propelled by the taught fishing line, broke entirely free and whizzed past my ear. In one, last, desperate bid, I punched my hand into the gills so far that I thought it might hit at my elbow. Then I ran. I ran twenty feet away from the river.

So, the first steelhead I caught did not even have a hook in it!

My second steelhead was easier, but it wasn't my fish, really.

Freezing weather had temporarily receded, as it sometimes does in the winter in the Pacific Northwest freezing one week and back up to 50 the next. I went to the Sandy. I was a veteran. I had proven myself. I had caught a winter steelhead.

I could not hook another fish to save my life.

Fairly close to Tad's Chicken and Dumpling restaurant, I found a small patch of open water and began casting a steelie. I read that steelhead could be caught on the Sandy River on large golden spoons, that Sandy River steelhead had a propensity for steelies, that those Sandy River Steelhead were vulnerable to glitter. I believed everything I read about steelhead. The trouble was that steelies used to come twelve on a card, and that stretch of the river below Tad's is the number one most snagy hole I have ever seen. It's worse than under the bridge at Dodge Park. It's snaggier than One O'clock Rock on Eagle Creek. I had no idea what I was doing and how many steelies I would need. I was a retailers dream come true.

Right away, first off, I lost my magic green-frog flatfish. I should have known when I spotted what looked like a fishable area on the Sandy, that there was something wrong with that stretch of river, for there weren't any cars jamming the pull out. Why not? Well, the reason was that no one could actually fish that hole. Oh, you could pull a lure part way through it. But fish it? Only one man could. It was good for me that he showed up.

He watched me snagging and offered some advice. I assured him that I had caught a fish just last week, and I really knew what I was doing. He offered more advice. I showed him a picture of the fish. He went to fishing.

After a few casts behind a rock that I hadn't tried, he hooked a bright and healthy male.

We talked about the fish, and I admired its color. He said that it was his birthday, and he could only stay a little while. He had to hurry home for his birthday party, but that if he caught another he would give me the male. I opened my mouth to tell him, again, about my prowess as a fisherman- and to refuse his offer- but my mouth just said, "Oh, yeah. That would be great!" And then I added a, "Thank you."

Then I went back to snaggin' rock. He went

back to catching fish. He was good at it.

Apparently, he had been fishing that hole since he was a little boy. I had only been fishing a few months- total, aggregate, all together, and only one hour in that hole. I was pleasantly surprised to hear myself accept his kind offer instead of trying to be macho, and stupid, and talk myself right out of his good graces.

A few minutes later, the young man did hook another fish, a mirror image of the first, but after bringing the second fish in, he began to get very quiet. Of course, he was re-thinking his offer of giving a fish away. Only a steelhead fisherman would appreciate his offer. Give a fish away? Since that day, after I learned how to catch steelhead, I have had men beg me for steelhead, grown men plead for one of my fish. A few years ago, an older gentlemen was murdered for his steelhead on a nearby river, and this unknown young man had offered to give me a fish just because it was *his* birthday?

He picked up his fish to leave, and I kept my face to the river. I knew I would never see him again. He knew it. We would not be friends. It was simply going to be a one time act of kindness that I would never repay. I made a cast to a likely looking snag and prayed for a clean retrieve. It wasn't.

Without a word, he gently set his first fish on the grass and silently walked up to his truck carrying only one steelhead.

I yelled a thank you, but it seemed odd. How could a simple thank you be enough? But it was enough for him. What a neat guy.

So, if you are a volunteer fire fighter, and you gave a fish away some thirty years ago on the Sandy River- drop me a line. I owe you one.

Getting Priorities Straight

Some fishing days are frustrating. And this day was a hummer. It's funny, but I find that it is sometimes difficult to identify the goal on a fishing excursion. Betsi thinks our times on a lake are centered on romance, on the kayaks, on the beauty of the water, and on the surrounding scenery- on the existential grandeur of the experience together. But I always thought that it was about the fish.

My nephew summed it up once, "Catch 'em. Cut their heads off. And eat 'em!" Kial will no longer speaks to his grandfather, but I think of him often- every time I catch a little trout.

While I'm no longer much into killing fish, I'm all for catching 'em, and releasing 'em, after a close up and personal moment between the two of us- which means showing off and bragging to anybody around. It's a personality fault.

Betsi and I arrived on Goose at our usual late hour and ate lunch in the car watching the occasional wind gusts rippling across the surface of the lake. We had our windows down, for it was a good, warm, mid-summer day. My father would have said it was too sunny for fishing artificials on the surface. And he was correct, the way he fished them.

From the window of the truck, I watched a

few boats on the lake trailing worms and bait down low in the deep-water section of the lake. Betsi and I munched on our lunch and watched; they were catching fish in the deep water, so I was encouraged, because if fish can be caught fairly regularly on worms and little spinners- I would just kill 'em, figuratively speaking, with artificial surface flies. Betsi was encouraged because the wind seemed to be ebbing.

Arriving at lunch time is the worst. I should learn to stop for lunch somewhere on the mountain before we get to the lake, because it is difficult for me to calmly eat lunch while being so eager to push that kayak out into the water and get my fishing on. It reminds me of Christmas when my mother would insist that we read the Christmas story from the big, white, family Bible. I didn't have any trouble with the story of Christ's birth, it's just that I always wanted to get those presents on. There must be a moral, there, somewhere. By the way, I still have a couple of those early Christmas presents: a little red car (the forerunner of the match box cars- but made in Japan) and my Gene Autry chrome-like six shooter. I don't know what happened to the family Bible.

When we did shove off in the kayaks, Betsi was fast up the shoreline towards the north shore; it's her favorite. It's my favorite too. The wind usually doesn't hit the north end of the lake, and the water is shallow but still holds lots of pretty respectable German brown trout.

To fish artificial flies on the surface, the water should be shallow so the fish will see the artificials on the surface. That sounds simple, but it is a very important concept to grasp. While it is true that an occasional fish who spots an offering will rise an incredible height to take a well presented fly, deep water fish don't usually pay too much attention to the surface. We fly fishermen are just lucky that some fish actually look up. The trick is to find shallow water that holds fish, but shallow water does not usually hold good fish. Goose is different. Goose is special. Half the lake is shallow, but half the fish love it that way. I have never seen a lake like this lake.

Small, fish inhabit the west side of the lake tight up against the shore. The larger German brown trout take over the rest of the lake.

Those particular browns are the most vicious of the trout family I have ever encountered. For the most part, they do not simply strike a fly. The do not softly inhale and then fight politely on the end of a five weight floating line. Nope. They hit a fly like they think the fly might bite back. It is them or the fly. I mean, those browns hit a fly like a freight train running head on into another freight train! They hit like a summer steelhead on steroids. It's like they are swimming away from the kayak when they hit. Whammo! You better be holding your rod tightly.

Contrary to what you might think, it's not real imperative that a man know much about fly fishing to score big on this lake. I rarely fly fish in the traditional sense. Real fly fishermen snort at my technique. I see them on the lake, casting and casting, beautifully fanning the air; it is a wonder to behold. Sixty, seventy, eighty foot casts- big, ballooning back casts of which Roderick Haig-Brown would be proud.

I row the kayak around rather aimlessly and

trail a fly.

That's it.

Wish it were more complicated than that. I seldom cast. But I hook an enormous number of fish! All that time those real fly fishermen are casting and casting and casting- my fly is in the water. Fish are in the water. There's a certain logic to that, somewhere.

Right away, Betsi took off for the north end of the lake, but I'm usually a couple hundred yards behind her by the time I push off and get going. She's just quick and determined and knows just what she wants, for the north end is the farthest from the campground and away from all the bank anglers. Mostly, we have the north end to ourselves or an occasional small deer and a few eagles.

Just off the boat launch, there are a few dozen left over dead trees from some ancient time when the water was lower. Swallows inhabit the snags, and it's fun to watch them dive out of a hole high up in one of the snags and play Charley Ryan back and forth through the lonely old forest. When there are young swallows in the holes bored into the snags, I can hear the little fledglings cackling and calling to mom and dad for a few more grubs or midges. The way the swallows dart back and forth like the one and only fighter pilot I know, you would think they were going after mosquitoes, but Goose doesn't seem to have many mosquitoes. The air is just filled with a tiny white midge, cortus margaritas. Nobody who reads *my* books knows Latin, so I might be a letter off in that spelling and who would know? Cortus margaritas is a very small, white, fury looking little midge-like flying insect. There's just about a million of these little midges darting back and forth like Charley used to do, and the fish love them.

Occasionally, I will try dragging a fly through the snags, and while that can often be highly productive water, I'm usually trailing Betsi. While it is true that we are not joined at the hip while kayaking, I do try to stay in the same general quadrant as her. So, I skirted the snags and rowed nearly beyond them before letting out the fly line.

The first fly I thought about trying was a Royal Coachman. Funny that. Actually, a coachman is just about the only fly I have in my box. Left over from a previous fishing trip, and still rigged up on my fishing pole, was a store bought #12, and I just left it on the business end of my five weight floating line. During the winter, I had purchased a couple dozen of the small flies on ebay for some insanely cheap price, and they work mighty good on browns, but most often I will drag one of my own #9s. I have finally been successful at tying some of the smaller #12's, and I feel pretty good about that, but I lost all of my own smaller ones in the lilly pads and reeds a couple trips ago. The moral, here, is exceeding simple. Don't fish the lily pads and reeds.

Nearly immediately, the wind pushed me up close and personal with the last of the snags, and my fly caught and snapped right off. I couldn't find that fly after quite a few minutes of examining the old, dead tree and finally just tied on one of my own larger #9s. I feel a little smug about it when I fool a good size cutt with a feather and some superglue.

A #9 won't float up high on the surface film

but plows a little wake just under the surface, and I have come to believe that a fly trolled along just under the surface is not a bad thing. It's pretty productive, actually. It's more difficult to visually track a subsurface fly than a floating one, but it works out pretty good anyway for such a lazy fisherman as I am. If I found a more difficult way to fish for trout, I surely would not do it. I have never understood that mind set. It's easy, really. Stay out of the lily pads, and keep the fly in the water.

    I wasn't concentrating on the fly as much as on trying to keep an eye on Betsi so as to end up in the general area she was inhabiting. I was fairly confident that a fish would not strike my fly until I got to the old snag on the shoreline- the one with the arm sticking out to the lake- the one in which the eagle is so often perched. I remember the first time I saw that eagle sitting on the pointing arm. His head was bent forward, and he was concentrating as only a bird of prey can. It was clear to me that he was looking for fish, and if a bird can see a fish from a tree on the shoreline- there must be shallow swimming fish in front of that tree! See? Simple. What I found was that just in front of that old tree, the bottom of the lake changes from about fifteen feet to five. When the fish come up out of the deep water to the shallows, the eagle catches a glint of the fish, and if the fish does not hug tight to the bottom, if he makes a fatal mistake and swims up near the surface- that eagle is on it like yesterday! Through eons of time, how many fish have been caught by an eagle off that branch? I don't know. That, in itself, is a noteworthy question.

So, I trail a fly, back and forth, in front of that old snag. Simple.

As the kayak passed before the snag with the arm pointing across the lake, I readied myself, placed the reel firmly between my legs and rowed quietly on. The fly was trailing a good seventy feet behind the kayak when the fish hit. It was a strange hit, a mite softer than the typical grab and murder it. The fish hit short, and the fly popped to the surface. A quick check showed no problems with the fly or the line. Nevertheless, I sharpened the hook and threw it back out. As it hit the water fifty feet astern, another fish hit the fly. Again, short.

I brought that Royal Coachman in and replaced it with another. Betsi came over and tried to console me. I just smiled rather ruefully, and threw the fly over the side. A little breeze had come up, so I let the kayak drift across in front of the snag and then rowed it back again, but this time there were no takers.

Fish were rolling and jumping all around me, so I rowed slowly to the west along the reeds. The water looked to be about three feet deep, and at any time I could see eight to ten lunkers swimming about. Goose is a fantastic lake! Too many fish, it would seem, and yet they never turn up stunted but always good sized with some honest lunkers mixed in just to keep it fun.

After a few minutes, I had another short take. Those short strikes were puzzling me? I reeled in the fly, and it was perfect. Well, I told myself, if they are reluctant to take the #9, perhaps a store bought #12 would be just right. I reasoned that if the nine was just too big, for whatever reason, a #12 should slide right down. Right off, another fish hit short- even on the smaller #12.

I anchored the kayak on the north end of the lake tight up against the reeds. Betsi came over to check up on me, and I told here what was happening. Why, she asked? Her question was funny. Who knows the thoughts of a fish? The same fish were in the lake today as last week, and those same fish were hitting short, today? "I don' know," I replied. "But I've lost several fish- all short takes."

She's a funny woman. After giving all of about a half a second's thought to the problem, she took her paddle in her hand and dug away with a, "Put on a trailer hook."
I watched as she flew off skidding across the surface of the lake as cute as could be and as right as rain.

We used to do that on Puget Sound when fishing for king salmon after dad purchased a film about how salmon hit a lure. Time after time, in the film, we watched as salmon would approach a herring and snap their teeth, like a dog, at the herring from six to eight inches behind- as if they were trying to scare that little herring. We started dropping a hook ten inches behind the herring, and our hook ups tripled immediately.

I gazed over at Betsi paddling away out of sight and around the bend in the lake. "It will work," I whispered to her. "That will work."

It did. I tied a dropper an inch behind the coachman, and the next fish hooked solidly. The second fish hooked solidly.

I cruised back and forth in front of the snag a

few times and finally gave up and just drifted on the wind. There is a little trick I use in mid lake. With only a few feet of line out, I just bounce the fly along the surface by simply lifting and dropping the tip of the fly rod- just splashing the fly on the surface. Apparently, fish don't care about the kayak's proximity to the bouncing fly. Fish, large fish particularly, respond to this method. But you have to be quick. It's best to pool ten or twelve feet of line on your lap, when doppling flies so close, because when a large brown hits he will tear the leader apart if you don't give him slack immediately. Not in a second or two- right now.

The wind had blown my kayak nearly half way across the lake- way out into the deep water- before the first fish hit the bouncing fly. The fish left the water on the take and flopped back down into the water with a pretty fantastic splash that made other fishermen turn and take notice. Sixteen inches, if he was six, and full of fight. He just took that fly and headed back against the wind. After the slack line was exhausted, the fish continued to take line off the reel. Finally, when I had what I estimated to be about half the line out, I lightly palmed the spool and began slowing the fish down. With enough line out, I could put my hope on the elasticity of the line and mono to stop the fish without breaking off. But stopping the line did not stop this particular fish. He just began pulling the boat... up wind! That was fun. I looked over to Betsi to see if I was sufficiently impressing her, and saw that she was slowing working her way in my direction.

After a few minutes, the fish stopped its mad

rush to escape on the surface and sounded. Then he rushed the boat. Rushing the boat is a favorite trick of browns. They run madly back towards the boat hoping the line will go slack, and then they can jump and throw the hook. I view a rush as a very advanced technique… for a fish. Many of the fish in Goose have been hooked multiple times, so they get a little savvy. I reeled in like crazy, but it is impossible to reel fast enough to keep up with a madly rushing large brown. The best one can hope for is that when the line finally gets tight again, the hook has held.

After a few minutes of fight, and a couple smaller runs, I brought the fish to the net, held it up for Betsi to see, and then lowered the net back into the water. I tried to carefully remove the hook from the corner of the brown's mouth, but those fish have the sharpest teeth! It is usually a few days after an outing on Goose that I finally remove the last of the remaining teeth from my thumb and fingers. But, hey, perhaps there is another one of those morals there- something about don't play with fire if you don't want to get bit, or something like that.

I took a camera one day when I took out my old wooden boat that dad and I had built when I was twelve. But somehow, that old boat went under water, and I had a bit of a struggle swimming it over to the shallows where I could bail out the boat with my lunch cooler. It was very special to look down, into the water, and see the camera that I use for appraisals sitting on the boat seat *under* water. Since that day, I have decided to leave the camera at home, or the boat, or both.

This would be the end of the story, but if you happen to have the holster to a two gun Gene Autry set- let me know.

I'm also in the market for a new water-proof camera.

Betsi thinks our times on a lake are centered on romance, on the kayaks, on the beauty of the water, and on the surrounding scenery- on the existential grandeur of the experience. I guess she is correct, after all.

Up the Clackamas River

Any good fishing trip, any fishing trip that you want to start successfully, any fishing trip that has a hope of being exciting and rewarding starts out early, before the break of day. I'm not talking about the afternoon jaunt down to the neighborhood lake or river, but the one that demands a long drive in the dark, a trip where you can watch the sun lighting up the eastern sky, a trip that starts with a cup of hot coffee and a donut.

The donut part is essential. It reminds me of my virility, of my years in a patrol car. If you can't swing a donut in as the trip starts, lacing the coffee with rum will work. In fact, both are recommended by a some writers. Of course, I would not suggest that rum thing, but some people have seen it happen. They put lemon fillings in donuts. What if they put rum fillings in donuts? If Dunkin Donuts had done that, they would still be in business in Portland.

As I left the curves and started into the straight away near Eagle Creek, the lights in the roadside homes were just lighting up, and I had a momentary change of heart. Would it be so bad to stop and peek into the hole at the head of Eagle Fern Park? I know that I had planned to fish the Clackamas, but Eagle Creek is a pretty little stream if you get there early enough. Oh, the creek is truly picturesque all day, I am sure, but it looses a little something after the crowds arrive.

I found the park gate locked, due to the early hour, and parked outside the fence in a spot barely wide enough for the Subaru. There wasn't much parking room, but just enough. In truth, there wasn't enough room, but I knew the walk was only a couple hundred yards, and the one consolation was that I would probably hear the collision. I like the car enough, and I really shouldn't have parked on that tight little shoulder, but I was on an adventure, and the steelhead were running. Besides, the car was sticking so far out into traffic that it would be safe. If you park far enough out into traffic, people drive around the car and curse at you for being so dumb, but if the car is safely parked on the side of the road you never know what fool driver might clobber it.

As I approached the Corner Hole, the sky was finally brightening, and my heart was pumping. It was fishing time. The temperature was a good and steady thirty five degrees, so the water would not build up on the guides, and I'd taken enough of the donut filling in my coffee not to worry about ice building up on me.

I ran a large fly through the hole several times, up in the head where the white water spills into the pool. On the third, or fourth cast, nothing took hold, but I saw a tail in the water. I cast again, and again I saw a tail, but did not have a take. The fish was lying so tight against the head of the pool that it was easy to imagine the fly passing right over his head unseen.

I changed to a different fly and stepped lower down the hole and directly below the fish. Then I waded into the chilly water up to my knees. To have a chance at that fish, I would have to cast directly up river and strip the line back towards me. It looked impossible. Artificial flies are made for tail outs- any water where they can be worked around, next to, or above rocks or logs. They perform well dragged near to a submerged log or an underwater rock. In deep water, at the head of a pool, they just can't be worked correctly. Sometimes, they can be hung suspended in the white water or even skipped on the surface- if they can be worked from directly above the hole- but this hole had a tree in the water above the hole. There was just no way, I could figure, to throw a fly into the very head of the Corner Hole.

The cast was good, up in fast water above the hole just short of the downed tree, and as soon as the line hit I began a super fast retrieve, but the fly was fairly racing down the current straight at me. I furiously pulled line. As fast as I stripped the line, the fly got ahead of me and tumbled lifelessly into the white water at the head of the pool.

The cast was good.

The retrieve was rotten.

The presentation was hideous.

The fish was hooked solidly deep in the corner of his mouth.

That cast had been followed by the worst line retrieval imaginable. That's probably what saved the day, for me. The fish looked at that artificial and thought that it had to be a genuine, edible insect for the sole reason that nobody could deliver an artificial so sloppily. He was a smart fish, that. It was a little like my parked car. That cast was so out of the ordinary and so downright stupid, that the fish just had to notice it.

It was a small steelhead with more spots than anything else. It looked more like a large cutthroat than a sea-run rainbow, but I knew they had been coming small that year. The fish jumped a couple times and ran right past me to the foot of the pool. I jumped a couple times and ran to the foot of the pool. There really is no bank down river from the corner hole, so, of course, that's where the fish went, and I couldn't turn him. I strained the tippet but finally gave up on the idea of turning the fish and just started following as best as possible. If you have ever chased a steelhead down a rapid chute of water with no bank and with overhanging branches in your way, you know just what I did; I raised the rod high in my left hand and went from overhanging branch to overhanging branch with my right hand. The footing was terrible. I stumbled and fell, stumbled and fell, and grasped at hanging branches like a… crazy man trying to run down a small river after a wild and thrashing fish.

Inadvertently, I was keeping pressure on the fish. With my rod high in an attempt to avoid tangling around a mid-stream rock, the fish tumbled downstream. He had to pull against the line, and somehow my tight rod tired him.., somewhat. I know it tired me. At the Small Log Hole, he pulled out of the current to rest. I think we were both too tired to try the next stretch of fast water. After a couple desultory runs of only about ten feet, we came to each other's feet on a small sandy shoreline. The hook came out rather too easily, so I guessed that I was lucky it held as long as it did. What a story he had to tell, for I let him go back to his arduous journey.

I was a little wet and beat up from the skirmish with the overhanging branches and the loose and shifting footing, so I made my way back to the Corner Hole and caught my breath on the picnic bench that overlooks the pool. I was still breathing hard, but I took out my pipe and lit it up, anyway. I'm not really sure why I light up a pipe once every year, or so. I don't really enjoy it. I enjoy the flare of the match and the first pull, but not the smoking of it. I imagine that I make a dashing figure alongside a cold, mountain stream while I exhale big, billowing clouds of blue smoke. But it tasted awful! I guess I do it because dad did. Somehow, if I do little things like he did, perhaps he's not really gone.

After a few minutes, I thought I saw another movement in the hole, up in the head where I hooked the earlier steelhead. Unconsciously, I set the pipe down on the bench and stepped closer to the little cliff that overlooks the foot of the hole. It was pretty hard to tell if it was really a tail? A steelhead is a pretty difficult fish to see in the water, even in a perfect situation, and there was so much white foam that I just could not be sure.

It was just like a Smith and Wesson .38 caliber handgun.

The rule I lived by, when I was working the street as a police officer was- when faced with an unknown situation, when something was not right, when I just could not be *sure* if I should draw my sidearm from its holster, or not- that was when I should fill my hand with iron. That day, looking at the

Corner Hole, I just wasn't sure if that was a fish's tail I was seeing. I just could not make it out clearly, the shadowy image came and went in the water. Whenever the water would clear, for a second, I thought it might be a tail. Then again, it might not. So, I obeyed my rule. I wasn't sure- so I filled my hand with fishing pole, pulled that rod back.. and fired another cast.

The cast wasn't as good as the previous one that led to the hook up before, for the fly rode the current and missed the head of the pool. I pulled the line up and looked at the fly. It looked good, so I tried again. The second cast was a trifle more into the current, but I lost sight of the fly immediately. Nevertheless, when I figured the fly was just about where it should flop into the head of the pool, I let the line go slack. I know that was the wrong thing to do. My only excuse is that somehow it felt good at the time.

Of course the fly snagged.

But, of course, that snag pulled back.

What a wonderful little side trip that was. *I will just stop and see how the Corner Hole is on Eagle Creek*, I had told myself. Well, I saw how it was. It was just fine!

Just after I released the second steelhead, two young men walked up.

"Any luck?" one asked.

"Oh, yeah. Two fish."

The first young man looked at my fly pole and sneered. "Uh, huh. Is that your car parked in traffic?"

What could I say?

I left with a light step and a song in my heart.

I had hooked two steelhead in less than twenty minutes before the sky was even at full light.

So, if you get out to the Corner Hole this season, there are two things I would like you to remember. Look for tails in the head of the pool, and take a look on that picnic bench for me, would you? I miss that old pipe.

A good and successful fishing trip starts with watching the sun lighting up the eastern sky, a trip that starts with a cup of hot coffee and a donut.

Up the Clackamas River Again

After dinner, Betsi thought it was only fair that if I was again going up to the Clackamas River in the morning, I should first take her for a walk in the cool of the evening- not too far, just around the neighborhood. And in truth, it turned out to be a fun walk, as most things are with Betsi. We took a couple hotdogs to feed to Cruz and Bear but neither answered to our calls. We figured they were probably inside watching TV with Rick, so we left the dogs on the grass just over the fence. I would have been inside our own home watching TV, if I hadn't been on a walk with Betsi. Ours was a better choice, I think.

Betsi informed me that I was not getting a donut in my coffee that evening, because I drank it all in the morning when I went up to the Clackamas River- where I did not go, she reminded me again, and who do I think I am going fishing two days in a row, anyway? I had no retort. When women use logic, on us men, there is not much hope.

It is true that I do not deserve a second day in a row of fishing, but she smiled and said that it did not bother her in the least, my going to the Clackamas River if I write a story about it, and if I publish it in my next book, and if people buy the book. If I could guarantee all those things, then she didn't feel at all irritated if I went to the Clackamas River, at first light. That was really good of her. Cause I was going. The steelhead were running. But I did go to the donut store before I went to bed.

There are very few guarantees in life; I can't *guarantee* her that any of my books will sell. They do, but that is not why I write. I write because I must, for my own something-or-other deep inside that compels me. For the first twenty five years of writing, I did so without publishing. Now that I'm in the big time and publish my books- I am impressed by the whole thing. My books are very useful. I have a whole line of them on the mantle over the fireplace. At Christmas time, they hold down that funny looking little white lacy stuff women think looks like snow. As for sales, after all my relatives and all our friends at church buy a copy of my newest book, I notice that sales fall off pretty sharply. If I had more children, or our church would grow, I guess I would make a lot more money.

In the morning, I left early and Betsi was there to hand me the thermos and give me a goodbye kiss. Truth be told, she was looking forward to a second day, in a row, to do her own thing, which I suspect will be a general field day of the house and another screening of *An Affair to Remember*. Fancy that, will you, she gets a day off and thinks it's fun to clean the house? I am one lucky man.

I laid the thermos on the passenger seat and backed the car out the drive careful not to hit any of the neighbor's cars. If I did, they might accuse me of having one too many donuts in the morning. The drive was a remake of yesterday, and, once again, the sky began brightening as I sped through Eagle Creek. I thought of the Corner Hole on Eagle Creek and was tempted to check it out, once again. But a promise is a promise, so I stayed on the highway.

Besides, if you ever have one of those marvelous days on a river, if everything you try works out, if there are willing fish, if it's a ten out of ten- don't go back the next day. Glorious days are like lightning. They never strikes twice in the same place. Well, lightning does sometimes strike twice in the same place, and that, I guess, is what keeps us going back, after all.

The North Fork Reservoir was just absolutely stunning in the morning light, with the sun glittering off the water and a light mist concealing the opposite shore. The road up the Clack was deserted, lonely, and deceptive. Often the road along the Clackamas gives one a feeling of being alone, of being secluded, but park alongside the highway and you'll get your doors blown off in just a few seconds. There are fewer people in the winter, of course, because the road is snow-blocked a few miles up, usually at about the Collawash River or sometimes closer to Ripplebrook Ranger Station, but there is always a car from somewhere speeding to somewhere else more important than where the driver left from- and on this particular road drivers fly. Sometimes I stop along the road and watch them zooming one direction and then the other. I sometimes, think they should all just stay home, but then- I'm on the road looking for an interesting somewhere zooming past some other guy who's eaten way too many donuts and might just be thinking of writing a book.

I pulled over above Lazy Bend Campground. The river is brushy, and one must spend a few years learning where the best holes are. Some steelhead fishing holes, don't look much from the highway, and I remember when I first started fishing here in the late seventies- I had an unusual method of finding fishable water; I would park where I saw other cars pulled out. That might have worked better for me than for all those other souls looking for a lonely fish or two, and I hope they will forgive me now, but I was trying desperately to learn a new river and a new fish, and a new method of fishing. They were all new to me, the river and the steelhead.

This day, the river was flowing just about perfect, if a little too clear for most steelhead fishermen, but I like it clear, the clearer the better. I like it warmer, though; the thermometer in the car read a chilly 36, with a forecast to dry out, warm up a little, and with sun breaks in the afternoon. My son, Chris, is a professional weatherman. I took my raincoat.

The temptation is to wade out too far into the water, in the hole above Lazy Bend. I had to remind myself, to just be content to wade to the big rock and stay there. I can't fish the entire river, but the temptation is always there to try. Really, anyone who wants to fish more and better water than the large sweeping run above Lazy Bend just wants too much out of life. And anyone who wants to wade further than the big rock, well, God bless 'em. I already fell in that hole once. Not that you can drown in the

Clackamas in too many places, but you can sure get wet.

It's not true that you can't drown in the Clackamas River. It has some verifiable class 4 water. Don't fish where it is dangerous. Simple. One can't drown in the fishing holes I fish. I have a long-time standing rule about potential trouble on a river- don't go there if it's trouble. If it is dangerous, I stay away. Sounds chicken, doesn't it. It is. But let's think about that. Out on a river you are alone. No one knows exactly where you are. There is no one around for immediate help- just someone to find your lonely, waterlogged body once it finally comes to rest under a large tree trunk on the edge of the river. Even if you are fishing with a buddy, you are alone once you go under. I have been there, and I never want to go back.

One time, I fished the hole above Lazy Bend and waded in past the big rock. It was my first time with chest waders, and my last. For years, I had been watching fishermen with chest waders. I watched the videos of those in chest waders hooking up with large fish. I read all the books. I even read an article on the etiquette of wearing chest waders. After I parked on the highway and was just about blown off the highway by the obligatory logging truck, I managed to pull myself into my brand new chest-high waders which would take my fishing to a new level- where I could reach those elusive big ones- where I could find my utopia. I even tightened on a belt (as demanded in the chest wader etiquette article) around my waist. Ostensibly, the belt is in case you fall in; it will stop water from rushing in and filling up your waders- and drowning your poor stupid person. Right.

I ignored the big rock and moved past it like it wasn't there. Finally, I could cast the entire river, even reach the stretch across the river that always looked so fishy but could never be reached. I reached it.

Then my feet flew out from under me. That belt sure worked. It kept all the water out. It kept all the water out and all the air in, so the waders acted like a giant balloon wrapped around my poor stupid person. My legs were full of air and wanted to float. My head and chest wanted to sink because they were out of air from yelling for help. My legs shot up, and my head sank down. Now, there is a rule somewhere about keeping your head above water. It is more than a rule. It is a law, but try as I might I couldn't do it. Three times, I forced my feet to the bottom of the river. Three times, they shot straight up and put my head under water. That's what I get for ignoring a three thousand year old rock the size of a 1948 Plymouth.

So, if you fish the hole above Lazy Bend never ignore that big rock. I always step up onto it with reverence. That is why God put that rock in the river- to help save some poor stupid person with visions of grandeur. I don't *need* to fish the entire river. My side is just fine.

I took the waders back and told the guy in the store that two minutes after getting into the water, with those new boots, they filled up with water.

But before taking the waders back to the store, I changed into my old hip boots and then went back to the water and climbed up on top of that rock. It is an idyllic drift- the water runs free and clear a couple feet deep and then the river narrows and deepens in front of the rock. The depth is about four feet and flows about as fast as a man could walk if he were young and in a hurry. The bottom is strewn with uneven sized boulders. That is just about perfect steelhead water. Behind the rock, the shoreline is clear of trees and brush. It is as if that rock was made for poor, stupid guys like me who fly fish.

The fish must have followed the fly all the way along its arc. Maybe. Who knows what a fish does? It hit in the shallows in only about ten inches of water just before I gave up and was about to strip in the line. Nice little wild fish. It fought pretty tough for a seven pound male. Wild fish are a ten compared to hatchery fish. I never met a hatchery fish that rated over a six in fighting abilities. That's why they call wild fish.., wild. Who would have thought?

When I took a knee, I thought of dad and that wild hen up on the Skokomish River. Who could forget? I slid the buck back and forth in the current to make sure it was fully revived and pushed it free into the current. He hung, there, clearly visible for a few seconds, and then he was no longer. They just have a way of disappearing.

I plied that run every which way and did not see another fish. It got cold, so I went back to the car for my hidden stash that the wife doesn't know about. I tried hiding donuts, but donuts tend to stiffen up a little after a couple weeks. Rum in a bottle never does that. A little bit of that in my luke warm coffee, and I felt a little better, a lot warmer, and roaring for more action on the river.

There is a section of river, below that big rock, that cannot be fished from the bank. Well, perhaps it can, but not with a fly. It's brushy. The only place it isn't brushy is on another... large rock just below the primitive campsite. It's the second rock out into the river. You can't miss it. God chose those rocks carefully; if the first rock had been wobbly, the second rock would have been inaccessible, and a careful man like me could never get to it. Still, one cannot fish with a fly from either rock. It's bait cast only. But I only catch fish with a fly. What to do? What to do? I looked into the back of the truck, and Betsi must have done it- somebody did it. Someone put a Lamiglas medium-weight bait casting rod and an Ambassador bait casting reel back there under all my fly fishing gear and empty donut boxes.

Some people think there is an art to fishing a spinner in low, clear water. Roderick Haig-Brown thought so. There was a time when he thought nothing of casting a "shiner" as he called a large spoon that probably resembled today's steelie more than anything else. When he was a young man, he was not adverse to a spinner, and he enjoyed fishing it immensely. Well, I don't know who put that Lamiglas in the back of the old truck, but I enjoyed that spinner immensely all over that hole without a single strike. So, nothing has changed. Not one wit. I only *catch* fish on a fly.

Just as I was hiding the... uh, placing the Lamiglas back in the old truck, a Ford pulled up and a man even older than me got out and started putting on his chest waders. When our eyes met, he waved and then came right over. We shook hands and he asked me if I wasn't.., "that small-time writer, what's-his-name, you know, the fishing writer from Milwaukie?"

"Well," I replied, "that might just sum it up nicely."

That kind of chance meeting might be just what's needed, every once in a while, to kind of build up a mostly unknown author when he is down. Then the man at the river advised me that he loves my books, and reads them often. The short stories, it seems, are just the perfect reading length for his morning times in the bathroom.

    I moved on up the river to the bridge at Memaloose Creek. There is a law in Oregon prohibiting fishing from bridges. Strange law, that. That particular law has always struck me as something the Sheriff of Nottingham might pass. Anyway, off this bridge, one can look right down on resting steelhead and salmon. They come out of the deep, slow water and sneak over into the shallows under the bridge. They pause there, in plain view from above, for a while and then drop back to deep water or swim away upriver. Mostly, they hurry up to seek shelter in the shadow under the bridge. Most all of fish that I have seen, rush upriver to another deep and slow pool that I have never fished, but from the bridge, you can see if there are resting fish, and today I was lucky.

    Under the bridge, it's just about perfect water for throwing a fly. There is little brush impeding a back cast. For you fly fishermen who are like me and really only have one cast- and that one cast takes forty acres behind you- it's nice to get a break every once in a while from the brush behind. The current is just a mite faster than a healthy man in a hurry might walk. The water rushes over rocks and stones about the size that a landscape artist might call two and three-man rocks. Then the water drops into deep, green water where anxious steelhead stack up until the upriver urge becomes to great for them to refuse.

    The back cast felt good, and the line went tight as the fly settled onto the surface. Probably, I told myself, a dry fly won't even come close to enticing a strike. I was right. But I had to try. On about the fourth cast I tightened up on the fly as it began its sweep across the current. The fly bounced a few times and then started skipping across the surface and reminded me of dad's Polar Shrimp at Point no Point. Here it is. Wait for it. Whammo!

    You cannot hook a steelhead on a dry fly on the upper Clackamas River. It cannot be done. I did it. I surely did. The fish was a little unruly, since he had rested in the deep water, and he was fresh and mean. Immediately on taking the fly, he jumped and dropped back into the deep water where he jumped once more before sounding like a salmon at.., Point no Point.

    I worked my way past the boat launch and hurried to the tail of the deep water at the foot of Memaloose Creek. Successfully below the fish, I put just a little pressure on the fish to, hopefully, make the fish run up river, or jump, or something that would expend his energy. The pressure worked, and the fish moved into the current and headed for the bridge. He never got there.

    He did the funniest thing- which is what keeps me coming back. He fought and fought and then gave it up, all at once. But even then, he was a special fish; with his last ounce of strength he pushed himself up on top of a large stone along the side of the river! I met him for the first time high and dry and waiting for me like a turkey wanting his head chopped on top of one of those three- man rocks.

      He was a beautiful fish with deep maroon and pink all along his sides, and was missing his adipose fin, so I did the unforgivable up along side his head and took him home to Betsi.

      I like to fly fish for trout under the bridge at Memaloose, but I don't have much luck unless I put on a fly that sinks a little. A wet fly will consistently raise ten inch rainbows that are probably planted fish turned mostly wild. One day under the bridge, a young man was catching so many trout on worms, that it should be illegal. He was having the time of his life-which is about what you get for keeping as many fish as he put in his creel- life. He looked oblivious to a catch limit, so when the time was appropriate and I engaged him in conversation, it was like trying to reason with a dead stick. He was having fun, and that's all there was to it. After about the third time explaining to him about catch limits, he blurted out that unless a police officer came along and screwed a .357 in his ear- he wasn't about to give up his trout. I didn't.

      Upriver on the south side, there is a good hiking trail that follows along the river for quite a while. I don't know the length of the trail. It just keeps going and going, and I am always tempted to stop walking and try a good looking stretch of water, so I don't know how far it goes.

Once, on that trail, I stopped and fished from a large moss covered boulder about five feet above the river. Cast after cast the line was unmolested. The water was perfect, the light was wonderful, the weather was marvelous and warm, the air was sweet smelling. The fish were not interested.

So, I broke a long standing rule and looked in my fly box for something other than a Royal Coachman. In that box was a small bead-headed black looking little critter tied on an itty bitty little tiny hook- it was one of dad's #20 flies with a big name that only Leroy knows. It might have been a Pheasant Tail Nymph Bead... I think. If Leroy, my famous fly fishing friend, ever comes around I will ask him.

A ten inch rainbow hit on the first cast with the bead-headed thingamajig. Thanks, again, dad.

A river runs through it.

It is true that I do not deserve a second day in a row fishing on the Clackamas River.

Special and Secret Holes Revealed

The upper Clackamas River, above River Mill Dam, is closed to winter steel heading. The logic of the those in charge is based on the fact that nobody fishes it, anyway, so why not close it? Huh? Their basis for thought harkens back to several years ago to when nobody fished the upper river one season. One. The road was closed. Nobody in the fisheries department thought about that. Actually, it's Kevin Costner's fault. They were filming *The Postman,* and after a few weeks of fighting off weird tourists from Portland, they simply closed the road, so no one could get in the way of their filming. It's pretty hard to fish a river when you can't *get* to the river. I just want to yell that at the Department of Fish and Wildlife?

I love fishing the upper Clack. But the authorities would have been correct if they had said that very *few* fishermen attempt winter steelhead, there. Just me and about two other guys I don't know. I *guess* they are fishing when I see their trucks parked along the river and its twenty-nine degrees outside.

But winter, summer, or spring, there is a hole above Sunset Park Camp Ground that is marvelous.

It's one of those spots where you will just have to look for the hole, because it's not much to look at and difficult to describe. It's merely one rock to stand on. Park in the turnout just up river from the park. You will love the hole. It is picturesque. The entire river shallows out and drops into a deep hole in front of a great looking campsite. The hole is deep, has the correct speed for steelhead, few snags or obstructions.., and doesn't hold fish. Fish up above- just before it spills into the hole or, best yet, go down river a hundred feet through the thick brush and stand on the small gravel beach. The branches, behind you, will snag your lure on the back cast- unless I've been there first. If you find the branches all broken off- you owe me. If you are from the National Parks- I didn't do that.

Cast up river and let your lure or bait drift just your side of the big rock you will see under water. It's only about fifty feet out. The bottom is deepest just this side of that rock, and you will be able to tell that the main current sweeps through there tumbling over a few good size stones to hold a big fish. But watch downriver, because often fish will slide right up under your feet.

One winter, before the authorities got so wise that they shut the river to fishing, I stood on that rock and cast to the rock fifty feet out for about an hour. Nothing. The water was perfect, my delivery was outstanding, and nothing! I could not see a fish, and just thought I'd try it one more time before going up above the campsite. Whammo! Good word, that. It was a big fish, just a tinge of sparkling pink on chrome, and I held it to the sky and thanked God that

I, and not one of those other two guys, had caught that marvelous fish.

The trouble with this hole is that there is just no way to fight a fish if it leaves the hole and runs down river. That would be OK, except that they *all* run down river. It's bushes, tangled brush, and the water is deep. Good luck. You will have the time of your life chasing a fish down to a small landing area about six feet across. If you miss this spot, just smile and try to follow it further down river- but you won't be able. Save you mono. Just smile and say goodbye.

Up above the campsite, I was fishing one summer day. I had the entire river to myself. You will see a large flat rock just above the campsite. Stand on it. Then cast. I did. The fish hit just as the steelie dropped into the deep water right in front of the campsite. It was a great fish, all of ten pounds, and bright but with a lovely pink stripe down its side. He ran up river and then down, but I held him at the little sandy beach in front of the campsite and slid him up and onto the sand where we were both panting for breath and both pretty excited. I did a mash job on his forehead and hung him in a tree. What a fitting end to a wild acting steelhead! After three years fighting the Pacific Ocean and then evading the sea lions in the Willamette River, he made it all the way up past several dams and into the upper Clackamas River, his home water. Then I bashed in his head! Wish I hadn't, but I used to kill a lot of fish. No longer. I leave them, now, for those two other guys.

Back down on the Willamette, if you park at Meldrum bar, walk up from the parking area until you see a medium size tree root sticking out of the steep rocky bank. Cast there. The bottom is a fairly consistent depth all along that stretch of the river- except for in front of that root; it drops a couple feet in front of that snag and both salmon and steelhead tend to stack up in the deeper hole. They stop there to catch their breath and take a break from their constant struggle to gain a yard, here, and a yard, there. Don't let them do that! Hook 'em, kill 'em, and take 'em home and eat them! It's not green, but it's fun.

The mouth of the Clackamas is pretty good- well nominally, so. It would be good, except that soo many fishermen hit it so consistently, that they tend to either catch them all before I get there, or scare them all off, or I'm just no good at fishing that stretch of river. When I was first starting out, about a hundred years ago, I fished there and hooked a bright little steelhead. It would have helped if I hadn't broken that spin-n-glo off just before the fish hit. The best water is close to the bank on the north side just as the Clackamas turns into the Willamette. If you cast out more than fifteen feet, you are too far. The fish cut the corner as they enter the Clack. You will probably have to fight with the plunkers to fish this spot, but go ahead and try. Perhaps you will make a few friends.

It was icy and cold when I first fished that spot. There were big chunks of ice floating down the river. It was so foggy, that I could not see thirty feet, but I could hear fog horns every once in a while. I put on a red spin-n-glo and cast out ten feet. Two things happened at once. I snagged and reefed back on the pole in an attempt to free the lure, and a huge (I mean bigger than life) tug boat came instantly out of the fog not thirty feet away and blew that horn so loud I lost control and broke off. I admit to being scared. That boat came out of nowhere, sounded his horn, and brushed right next to me. It was an involuntary moment of fright that caused me to jerk back on the rod so strongly that the line broke. But I didn't run. I would have run, but my feet were frozen to the rock I was standing on.

The next instant, a chrome bright steelhead jumped- with my spin-n-glo in his mouth. The water was about a foot deep, ten feet from the bank, and a steelhead took the spin-n-glo deep in the corner of his mouth. "Who's fish is that?" asked the excited plunker to my left. "Well," I replied. "It's sort of mine, and it isn't sort of mine"

Guys in fishing boats set out in the river, there, and plunk for salmon and steelhead. In the deep and thick fog they have devised an ingenious method of not being run over and killed by the tug boats. They stand an oar on end with an over turned tin can on the top of the oar. That's all it takes for the tug boat radar to pick them up and avoid a collision. I think I will leave that to the boaters who love to anchor mid river and plunk for big fish in the fog. It was bad enough being on the bank when a tug boat came by. The first instant he loomed out of the fog, I thought he was pulling into the parking lot!

Dodge Park, on the Sandy River is a pretty marvelous place to fish. It used to be great. Don't we all get tired of hearing that?

Nonetheless, go to Dodge Park. Go there and fish mostly in season- right under the bridge. Forget about the deep green and beautiful water against the cliff. I know, it looks fishy, it looks as if a fish ought to love hanging out there. But they don't. Go under the bridge and stand on the only rock there. How's that for simple? Even I could follow those directions! Stand on that rock and look out about twenty feet. If you see a steelhead, cast to it. What could be simpler? Or more fun? Most fish, once hooked under the bridge, never run farther than the deep green and beautiful water against the cliff, because what the fish do like- is *fighting* in deep and beautiful holes. When they tire, bring 'em in and bash 'em.

The other place to fish at Dodge Park is nearly at the southern end of the park. There's one big rock standing hard in the current. Throw a steelie in front of that rock. Isn't fishing technical? Throw to it and try for the occasional fish that rests, there, in front of the rock. Not many do that, but once in a while I get lucky.

I did hook a gigantic salmon a little further down towards the confluence with the Bull Run River. In fact, it was exactly where the two rivers join. If I remember correctly, I stood on a rock and spotted a very large Chinook. So, I threw one at it. One what? You guessed it. That dumb fish took the steelie on the first cast and was hell bent on returning to the Pacific. Now, that's a particular problem, here, because of the Bull Run River you just can't follow a fish that goes south. What could I do? I fell back to my open bail trick and free spooled the line, and what do you know? That dumb fish stopped and came back right to the same rock where I had first hooked him. I was standing on that rock. This time I put pressure on him from down river, and he burnt leather going up river and away from the Bull Run. That was great, because then I could follow. And I followed him, too, for about a hundred feet when he decided to just leave. There really isn't much you can do with ten pound monofilament against a sixty pound salmon. The line parted, and I wished him luck. At least, that's how I'm telling the story, but after four years in the Marines and a few years with the Portland Police Bureau, I know how to swear.., artfully well. I'm not saying that I did swear at that primeval throwback, but I could have. I know some choice ones. My brother, Harold, would have said, "Dad, nab it!" but I never got the hang of that kind of talk, myself.

As to the Bull Run river, I have caught some wonderful sucker fish on it. Don't waste your time. Guys used to go up to the outflow from Roslyn Lake and throw eggs right up next to the out take- it was amazing how successful they were, but since it is illegal, now, I wouldn't advise it. But when George Washington was a corporal, I saw a few guys get lucky there.

Up river from Dodge Park on the Sandy River, it is mostly private property and unproductive water. If, however, you are the lucky chump who recently built a cabin just where the two forks come together about a thousand feet up from Dodge Park, call me. We might work something out for fishing rights. It's a lovely hole where the river splits and then comes back together tight up against another sandstone cliff. The water is two feet deep, four miles an hour, and covered with medium sized stones. It is perfect water for both steelhead and silvers. In these conditions, I put the steelies and the spinners away and throw out the small spin-n-glo because the spin-n-glo floats up like a corkie- which is what a spin-n-glo actually is- a corky with wings that spin around. It's deadly in shallow water where fish hold in the current.

Closer up, and tight up against the cliff, the fish lie in the breaks between the fallen sandstone chunks, especially silvers, but steelhead like it up against the cliff, also. If you get lucky, there is about a mile of sandy beach to land a fish. It's a great hole, but since the cabin came in, I've only snuck in there a time or two.

One time I was there, before the cabin was built, Larry Day and I were trying for silvers, and I hooked one on a spinner in between the fallen sandstone chunks. It was a great, strong, and jumping fish, but I lost it when the line went behind a river rock and snapped. I made up for it an hour later when Larry and I went under the Dodge Park bridge. What a fish that was!

Try Dodge Park. Or try up under Revenuer Bridge. But try fishing somewhere. You never know when it will be your turn.

If you own that cabin above Dodge Park, give me a call. I'm in the book.

The Wilson River

The Wilson used to be a terrific river. I get tired of saying that, and I get tired of hearing it. But what's a guy going to do? The fishing *was* better twenty years ago, but you can't fish in the past, and at my age I might not be able to fish in the future, so I just fish today. Day by Day. That's a song we sing in church. I think that's Bill Nylund's favorite tune. Besides, twenty years ago I was there on the Wilson When Bill Nylund was still in school with Betty and Patty. Twenty years before that, the old timers used to say that the fishing was better twenty years before! So, there it is. It just is what it is.

The Wilson is a small river. You can cast across it without more effort than it would take to flip the lure across the two lane road they call the Wilson River Highway. But it holds fish, lots of fish.., at the right time, under the correct conditions- and then only for a short day or two. The problem is that the river is not long enough. It's length is only about twenty miles, or so, and that lack of length makes the river height fluctuate wildly; one day it is low and clear, the next it can be high and cloudy, and two days later it's clear as a bell, again. This demands that the fish rush up the river when it is high and hide in the deepest holes when the river drops. It is just after it drops a foot or two from its high point, that you can catch fish, and lots of them. But a day later, you can't catch a fish for money!

    Twenty years ago, fishing the Wilson River with Larry Day, the river might not have been as good as it had been, but it was still pretty good. There were still fish, but only if you knew where and how. Larry had the good sense to ask me how to fish for steelhead, what gear to purchase, and exactly where to go. At a store in Oregon City named, coincidentally.., Larry's, he put cash on the counter and purchased a Lamiglas rod and an Ambassador bait casting reel. He filled his fishing vest with steelies. He then spent a week in his back yard learning how to cast with a bait casting reel- you cannot learn that skill on the river. Well, I guess you could. But you wouldn't. After that, we jumped into my Subaru and headed for the Wilson.

    Try to learn how to cast on a river, and you will be like Mark Wold. I looked back at him, and there he was on a tall rock in mid river. He had his fishing line wrapped around his entire body, and he was trying to extricate his six-foot five inch frame from ten pound monofilament while not loosing his balance. I almost lost my balance laughing so hard, just watching. Or, maybe, Mark was having such difficulties with a five weight fly line. I just can't remember, but the point is well made. Practice at home. Fish in the river.

I never fish further down the Wilson River than the gravel pit. It's all farm land with cows and a very particular Tillamook City smell below that, and I never have found fish down there, anyway, so I consider the gravel pit the last stop. Once again, don't fish the pretty water where everyone else does. That water was already fished out before you got there. It's a rule. Wade out onto the rock nearly under the bridge. There is no water, from that rock, that looks fishable, but I have never cared about that. Cast directly upstream right into the current and real like the place down under. Do that about twenty times, and you might accidentally snag a fish in the mouth. If you do, just jump up and down a few times, and then send me an email.

Captain Bob Schwartz wanted to catch a steelhead, once, so we took the long drive. I told him to stand on that particular rock and cast up river and reel like mad. He did. You should have seen how bright that fish was! It was like the chrome bumper on my old '64 Dodge Coronet! Bob was about the smartest man I have ever known, so it sure was fun to know something he didn't. I knew where to fish. We sure laughed a lot on the return drive to Portland.

Another cop from work, Art Burger, was complaining about not catching a steelhead for years, and I offered to take him down to the gravel pit. At first his eyes lit up, then he sat back in his chair and said, "Oh. I can't. I have a boat." It was like, "Do you walk to work or do you carry your lunch?" Who can understand logic, like that?

The first fish I hooked from that rock was a monster of about fourteen pounds. I know how much the fish weighed because I mashed him pretty good after the fight and put him on the scales up at the Wilson River store. He took the hook and jumped straight out of the water. There wasn't much else he *could* do. The water was so shallow that his options were few. He raced up river, and then he turned and headed into the deep water below the rock. That was good for me, and bad for him. It was my turn. He stayed in that deep hole in front of my rock until his strength gave out.

Across the river from the gravel pit hole are four or five houses on a short, dead end road. One of the homeowners was out digging in his garden and doing things that I should have been doing in my yard, but when he saw me fighting a large fish he came down to the bank of the river and watched in deep interest. When he saw me slide that chrome monster up on the rocks and dispatch him so eloquently with a river rock, the man's shoulders slumped, and he turned around to resume his gardening. He should have been cheering! Catching a steelhead is a difficult and tiring process that happens only now and then and more often then than now, the older I get. And now that I'm not a cop, anymore, it's about the only chance I get to do any mashing. The only consolation is that *I* don't get mashed much, anymore, either.

Way up river, just east of where there used to be a restaurant, there is always the Power Line Hole. For a few years I tried to live at this hole. I caught so many fish out of the Power Line Hole that I lost count.

One spring day, with the sun high in the sky and with absolutely gin clear water, I spied two large fish come up the rapids and nose into the tail out. I knew it was impossible to go for those fish, because I was standing out in the open with the sun shinning directly on me for all the world to see. But, why not try? I cast the steelie up river a few feet and let that spoon wobble down towards those fish. It was a perfect cast, and the spoon was a beautiful thing to see in the water. The front fish took it like the whole thing was a dream. She never left that pool, and I slid her onto the rocks and did the big M on the side of her head.

That was a fun fish, but the other fish, for some indefinable reason, had disappeared, so I took the dead fish up to the Wilson River Store and bragged it all over the owner. She was always fun to take a fish to, and she put my picture up on the ten most wanted felony board by the gas pumps outside of the store .

She and I were doing that on another fine winter day, when a state trooper saw the commotion and slammed on his brakes. He wanted to see my license and tag. As everyone knows, cops can sure ruin a good day. I know I ruined his day. I had a license and a tag.

Another time, I was walking out to the car with a fish when a state trooper was walking down to the river. We were good friends, he and I. Went to the same church. We had eaten at many a pot luck together. Our kids shared a Sunday School class. He said to me, when we met by the river, "Can I see your license?" I was going to hit him, but as everyone knows that is pretty much illegal, now. So, I showed him my license, and then I asked him for his State Police identification card. He just spun on his heel and walked off. I've never seen him, sense.

I saw a big elk down at the Power Line Hole, once, but I didn't cast to him.

One day I was at the Power Line Hole and just could not entice a steelhead, no matter what I tried. I cast and cast, I plead, I cajoled. I could not find a fish, but it felt like there was a fish somewhere nearby. It was like I had radar, and it was blipping mysteriously- like Frodo's sword would turn blue. I *felt* a fish. Wading out into the current above the large rock is always dangerous, but I was there to fish. The water spills over into the hole and just crashes into a huge rock mid river. I let out a small spoon straight downstream. Gradually, the spoon floated closer and closer to the rock. I was hoping there was a fish hiding in the white water and foam where the water collided with the rock and was forced to turn to the left. When that spoon finally worked its way backwards to the rock- Whammo!

When the spoon hit that rock, a fish hit that spoon, and the excitement knocked me right off my feet. That water was so cold. I sputtered and splashed and made my way slipping and sliding over to the side of the river. That is exactly what that fish did, too. He sputtered and splashed and made his way over to the side of the river. Ten pound mono is a wonderful thing. The lady up at the Wilson River Store put another mug shot up on the wall.

My favorite hole on the Wilson is a lot further

up river nearly at the closed water. Larry Day and I pulled off the road through the guard rail and parked in the trees. Ten seconds later, Larry opened the back hatch of his Volkswagen and we heard a crash on the highway. What we found was amazing. Not half a minute before, we were on that highway, and we didn't see anything. In those few brief moments, after Larry turned off the highway, sixteen elk walked out into the roadway. Simultaneously, an old Indian in an old Ford Galaxie decided to hit 'em. Don't know why, but he must have decided it was a good thing to do, at the moment. That Galaxie slid right through an entire herd of Roosevelt elk. Elk flew everywhere, but they are amazing animals. After being hit by a ton of Ford, those ton size elk just picked themselves up, brushed themselves off, and walked up into the trees. Amazing!

The Ford had seen better days, but I'm not sure it really looked much worse after hitting those elk. It was pretty much dented up all over from head to foot, but it looked like it might have been that way for a while. The trunk was held shut by some electrical wire, and there was no rear bumper. True, the elk had knocked out the front windshield, but that old Indian had been around. "Guess I'll just drive into town," he said through his whiskey breath.

I thought about taking him into custody for driving while intoxicated, but Larry grabbed me by the shoulder and reminded me about the fishing we had been pretty excited about. He said that the old Indian might have had enough troubles for one day, and his encounters with the elk had pretty much sobered him up. Only the smell of whiskey was left.

Larry reminded me that cops aren't supposed to arrest people for things that are already gone.

We walked down to the first hole as the sun came over the mountain. Well, it never really comes over the mountain on much of the Wilson. The canyon is too deep. But the sun did brighten up the hill tops a little.

Larry and I used to trade off casts. First he would cast to a likely looking spot, and then I would cast to the next. It was his turn. On his first cast behind a large rock in mid river, a beautiful hen hit that steelie like it was something a ten pound steelhead could ingest. It wasn't, but Larry mashed it on the side of its head, anyway. I told him that it wasn't really fair, since he was so much bigger than that poor fish, but he just smiled. He was pretty excited about fishing that hole some more, but after a half an hour more, in a ten foot long stretch of river, I told him that I thought it was kinda foolish to fish for something that was already gone.

What was really fun, at that hole, was that I caught a glimpse of a bit of drift boat along the shore- just pieces of a drift boat, small ones. Nobody could possibly hope to float a drift boat on the Wilson River up above Wilson Camp. Nobody. God bless them, whoever they were. Hope they survived. But that boat sure didn't. I turned over a flat ex-part of a boat, and the word Budweiser was painted on it. That might have been part of the problem?

Larry and I were separated when he went back to his vehicle with the fish, so I went up river to the next hole. Along the way, I threw the spoon in several small but fishy looking spots. It was a very pleasant and warm morning, a pretty rare start for a Wilson River day. The water was the clearest. You could see every rock on the bottom. That is great for the ambiance of the moment, but for steelheading it's not the best, the fish tend to hold up in deep pools and not move during daylight hours when the water is crystal clear. In a way, that's a good thing if you can figure a successful way to entice fish in deep water. The best I've found is just to fish as deep as possible and try to slow down the lure so that it hangs in the water as long as possible- but that's pretty much what I always try to do. One way to fish extremely deep water is from directly above the hole. I just stand directly up river and let that steelie or spinner work and work until a fish can't stand the flashing any longer. It's a fun technique, but you must to be willing to waste quite a bit of time standing in one spot. But then, if you aren't willing to waste quite a bit of time, you probably shouldn't be fishing, anyway.

It used to irritate Larry when I would catch so many more fish than he, but in fairness it should be remembered that I had been fishing for steehead for twenty years, and it was his first winter. He caught more fish that first winter than any two newbies should have, but he had a great teacher. I think so.

One day, we stopped on a rocky outcrop that stuck out into the middle of the current- almost an island. Before we both sat down for lunch, I threw out a spinner and just let it dangle in the current. It wasn't in the best and most ideal spot, but I felt better with my line in the water. I used to hate to waste a minute fishing time, I was so driven. We ate and talked and laughed about life and family. When we had finished lunch, that old Lamiglas took a sudden bend and bounced and bounced. It was a good thing I had jammed it so firmly between two large stones. It was a good fish, not quite eight pounds, and it made Larry's jaws tighten.

Larry saved my life, once, near the last bridge before the closed water where there is a large rock standing twenty feet above fast water just where the water tumbles into a quieter pool. It was cold that day, and there was a layer of ice and snow on that rock, but we decided that if we were careful, it still might be a good place to fish.

On a good day, it almost takes two people to fish that rock, because if a fish hits, you must free spool the reel and throw the pole off the rock to the person down below. I often fish that rock by myself. With no other person, I am in the habit of just throwing the pole into the shallow water below the rock and running around the rock and down to the river. That's a dangerous prospect, but I've done it numerous times and not lost one fish in the process. The reason it is so much fun is precisely because it's so heart stopping to throw away my fishing pole, something I value so highly, hoping the fish won't drag the pole into the deep water. It's a trip, I want to tell you!

Well, Larry and I were careful, but that rock was so slippery that I took one look into the fast water, slipped on the ice and fell. Without hesitation, Larry threw himself prostrate on that rock and grabbed the collar of my coat. At about the same time Larry grabbed my collar, my foot found the only two inch outcropping God built into that rock a couple billion years ago, and with Larry's help I made it back up to safe footing. I don't think I could have stopped myself without Larry's help, but he says that he was no hero, and I shouldn't, like, write it up in a book and tell people he is a hero. I promised that I would not do that.

A few minutes later, I hooked a steelhead under the lip of that rock. It was great. I threw the pole to Larry, and he brought the fish in. What fun the Wilson River can be!

I don't fish the Wilson River as much as I used to. The fish are still there, but the traffic on the Sunset Highway is just so thick and congested that I can't get home after all day on the river.

The Wilson empties into Tillamook Bay along with the Trask, and the Kilchis, and a river not very many people fish- the Tillamook River.

I tried to fish the Tillamook a couple times, but it's mostly private property and what isn't private is not good looking water. I suspect that those who do any good on the Tillamook know a farmer and throw eggs into a private hole by some friendly cow pasture.

The Kilchis is a pretty famous river, and it puts out a lot of fish, but it's a crowd-only river. If you like people, up front and personal, you will like the Kilchis. But you should be there when the fish are running! Well, you should have been there twenty years ago when the fish were running! Still, if people don't bother you, you might just love the Kilchis- about a million and a half people do.

The Trask is a different story. The Trask might be better fishing than the Wilson, and that's saying something. The only trouble with the Trask is that if you live in Portland you must drive down the Wilson River Highway to get to the Trask. If I could drive past all that wonderful water in the Wilson to get to the Trask- there would just be something wrong with me. It would be shrink time. The only time I am tempted to fish the Trask, which is a mighty fine steelhead and salmon river, is when I have driven the length of the Wilson and not had any success. What invariably happens is that if I haven't caught any fish by the time I get to the Gravel Pit- I'm a little worn out, and I know that if I go over the Trask and fish it I'll be dead tired on the trip back up the Wilson to the Sunset Highway. So, I usually just think about it and turn back up the Wilson River Highway- where every hole I fish on the way up the river is one mile closer to home. Sounds like the reasoning of an old man on the river- which is what I just about named this book, but you have to admit that it doesn't exactly stir up visions of adventure and fishing daring do. I might as well call it, Sometimes When Betsi is Not Looking, I Smoke a Pipe on the River. See what I mean. It doesn't sing.

The Wilson is a small river. You can cast across it without more effort than it would take to flip a lure across the two lane road they call the Wilson River Highway. It holds fish, lots of fish, but it can steal your heart if you are not careful.

Harriet Lake

Harriet Lake is a wonderful little twenty-two acre lake off the Clackamas River. It is thirty miles east of Estacada, and the drive parallels the Clackamas River for a good portion of the trip. The Clack is a gracious looking stretch of white water that holds an amazing number of steelhead and salmon, when they are in season. It holds them- real tight. The Upper Clack is known as a river with lots of fish, but it's hard to connect. In fact, it is such an stingy stretch of river that few people even try it.

Lake Harriet is at 2,000 feet in elevation, so while it isn't exactly a high mountain lake, it's not a flat-lander, either. It's a little bit like men my age. I am still young enough that women find me a threat, but I have trouble remembering just why.

If you drop down from the Mt. Hood highway and Timothy Lake, which truly is a high mountain lake, dropping down to Harriet is rather easy. Simply drive over the dam, on the west end of the lake and take either one of the two roads. If your wife washed your car recently, take the paved road to your right. It's six or seven miles to Harriet Lake. Both the paved road and the gravel road get to Harriet Lake- it's just that the paved road gets you there much cleaner. You can actually open your car windows and rest your arm out the window on the paved road. Try that on the gravel road, and well, you get the picture. If you care about the finish on your rig, turn right, and it's blacktop all the way… until you get to the cutoff-where the half a mile of gravel, just before the lake, makes the previous few sentences a little bit non-essential.

    The lake is owned and operated by Portland General Electric, and they do a great job of it.

    The rumor used to be that the lake had some monstrous brown trout. The rumor, today, is that the lake has some monstrous brown trout. It does. But you won't catch them. What you might be able to hook up with are some mighty nice little cutthroat in the east end of the lake and rainbows in the west. There are browns in the east end, but I wouldn't call them monsters. I would call them game fish worth the trip. Just.

    The first time I fished Harriet Lake was thirty years ago, with my three children. Of course, it was the children that made it special. It's a funny thing when you take children on an adventure; they are not aware that it's all for them, and if it isn't all for them-you made a mistake. It's all in the memories. You sure can't hold onto an old dead fish.

    It was summer. It was marvelous weather, and we found the last possible camping spot empty. I guess the camping fee was around five bucks, back then. I didn't complain about the cost, but it was high, for the times. The price for filling the tank on my

Dodge Truck was only ten dollars. The site backed up to the river and through the side windows of the trailer we could look at the lake. All in all, it wasn't too bad for a fiver. I don't know what it costs to camp at Harriet Lake, today, but it costs over a hundred dollars at the gas station if you try to fill up a big old Dodge truck. The hundred dollars won't fill the tank, of course, but that's all most gas stations will trust you for if you put it on your card.

  As I remember it, we had a little blow-up boat. It was yellow. It was nothing you could be proud of, but a boat you could dump a few kids into and not feel too guilty about taking them out onto small water. It got us onto the lake away from shore, and that is about all you could say about it- except that it was fun. There was something about being in a rubber blowup boat with two kids and some plastic oars. We laughed and rowed around, and laughed, and pretended to fish. It was just plain old ordinary fun.

  I wanted to fish. I always want to fish, but children have to play, and if you can't make them think fishing is fun they will never take to it. The lake was so shallow that I ended up taking all the weight off the line and just trolling a worm on a small hook. The nice thing about that was that with no weight on their lines they sure weren't going to be snagging on the bottom, and, fish being fish, the depth doesn't matter much with worms, anyway. If a trout sees a worm, it figures it's lunch. Worms, to fish, are like a cold beer to a guy on Saturday. Why *not* gulp it down?

  About the only thing that mattered to me was

the kids having fun. And that was easy, because the rule is with kids that having fun is synonymous with either making noise or eating. That's a rule. But the rule has to be tweaked just a little, because kids also get a kick out of anything squiggly- and nothing squirms and squiggles like a fresh caught rainbow trout. Just the possibility of getting slime all over them by a jumping, careening little rainbow was enough to set both children off. It's probably not a lot of fun for the fish, but the kids sure had a blast.

In the east end of the lake, there are numerous stumps left over from before the forest was flooded to make the lake. We found those stumps were great holding spots for ten-inch cutthroat. Of course, I stayed up on the east end of the lake because I had heard a rumor that there were monster browns on the east end where the creek spills into the lake. But, if one of your children hooks up with a big, healthy cutt every time you row past a large underwater stump, and your children hoot and holler the way Kevin and Jenny were hooting and hollerin', you don't really miss monster browns. After a while we went ashore and brought Chris into the boat, and those fish just did not seem to care who was holding the pole. That little tyke did just fine. Every time Chris hooked a fish, I wasn't sure who jumped the most or the highest.

I wasn't such a purist snob, back then, when it came to fly fishing. It was before my fly fishing days. I was a young dad, and it was worms and eggs, and screaming little children. Any day, now, I'd gladly trade the fly rod in for some screaming little ones, for fish die and go away and get smelly, and kids make that weird transformation to something other than children. I don't miss the fish smell, but I sure miss the children. I'd sure like to go fishing just once more with those three children before I die and go away and get smelly.

Years later, on the last day of the season in October, I took the trek to Harriet Lake. It was raining. Perhaps that is why I was the only one on the lake. It was cold too. It was still pre-fly fishing days, so I put on a worm and cast it into the creek as it rushed into the lake. I fished for a while with nothing much happening other than rain running down my collar, when I felt a tug on the end of my line. It was much like steelhead fishing. Something took the worm exactly like a lethargic steelhead in cold water. There was no mad dash, no aerial display. The worm simply stopped. I tugged on the hook. It tugged back. I never saw that fish. It tugged and pulled, and never came to the surface. After a few seconds, the line broke. Perhaps it was one of those monster browns everyone talks about, or it may have been the ghost of all those cutts the kids and I murdered years before. I don't know. All I know, for sure, is that we both tugged on the line a few times, and then we both went home wet.

Ten years later, a good friend and I risked our lives in a small boat dad and I built when I was in grade school. George Washington was still a corporal when we laid the keel- that part about George might be an exaggeration, but my grandfather had known a soldier from the Civil War when Abraham Lincoln was a corporal. In Harriet Lake, the boat was a tad bit too small for two grown men, but we tried it anyway, and we had to keep an eye to the bailing, for that old boat leaked just a bit. I don't remember why, but for some reason we ended up in the deep water on the west side of the lake where the logs cut you off from going too close to the spillover. Somehow, it made sense then. Sure. Two off duty cops in a dangerously leaky old boat ending up in the deep water next to the damn overflow. Sure.

"You catch a lot of trout, here, Len? Is that what you said?"

"There are some monstrous brown trout in this lake. You read that everywhere."

"Ever seen one?"

"Well, it was in print."

"Must be true," my friend admitted. "If it's in print."

My friend, Mark Wold, is a Clackamas County deputy, so he's naturally suspicious. I rowed him around until my arms were going to fall off, but he just couldn't connect with a fish. I hadn't had a nibble, either, but I had an excuse. I had to handle the oars. Mark's excuse was that the sound from all the bailing water splashing into the lake was scaring off all the fish. Finally, I just nestled up to the last log in the lake and told him about Tony Smith.

"Tony Smith?"

"Yeah. Tony works mornings at central precinct. He says he catches big fish, here, at the logs by the lake overflow."

"Ever seen one, here?"

It was about at that time that I leaned over and

looked down into the water to see if dad was watching. I saw one fish. Then I saw about twenty of 'em. They weren't big, but were they fun! For about an hour, we never even let line out. We would just bait up and drop the line over the side like kids with cane poles. We could see the fish, and they must have been able to see us in the bright sunlight, but as long as we kept feeding them scraps of worms they sure didn't care. It was a little tricky, though, because some of those fish were too small, so we would dangle that worm over the side and have to move it around to the bigger ones and try to avoid the little goldfish sized fry.

    The really big ones stayed out of harms reach and would not be tempted. Those were the real monsters. We could see them, but they would not move to the worm. Maybe they were browns. There are monster browns in Harriet Lake. You could almost hear them sneering at the younger trout going for worms. Worms on a hook!

    After a while, we began to feel a little guilty about all the easy pickins, and Mark was not sure if catching fish, like we were catching fish, was legal. Seemed to him that anything that productive must be illegal in some way. So, we took a few fish apiece and made for the launch, bailing all the way.

    Back at the launch a deputy sheriff was waiting for us. Seems he had been watching us catch fish left and right and wanted to know if we had current licenses, and all. I showed him my license, and Mark and I engaged him in meaningful conversations about fishing and hunting and fishing and hunting. We got that deputy to laughing and joking around with us until I pulled out my license and showed him my tag all over again, because I wasn't sure if Mark had a fishing license. I was sure that deputy could count. Two fishermen, and he checked two licenses. One Adam Twelve clear.

Ten years later, I hit Harriet Lake with a fly pole and a girl named Betsi who I had just happened to marry up with. We were in brand new kayaks that you didn't have to bail, and she was sure more fun than Mark Wold. Of course, I made off for the log jam at the end of the lake right off, with Betsi in tow. In those days, she liked to stay close as long as I didn't start grousing about one thing or another. We didn't have to bail, but there weren't any fish on the west end of the lake, either. Given the choice, I'd rather bail.

I was just about to flip a fly to 11 o'clock when a fish broke the surface under the trees on the south side of the lake. With a last drastic change of plans I put that fly at 3, right under those trees and hard up against a log where the fish had engulfed something tasty off the surface. He hit my fly immediately. He wasn't one of those giant browns, but he was a game little cutt that did good things for my esteem in front of Betsi.

We spent the rest of the afternoon back near the stumps on the east end of the lake where I picked up a few cutts and another brown for dinner on some store bought Royal Coachman. It wasn't easy pickens, but as long as I kept the line tight and kept flaying the water with that floating line, I picked up a strike every half hour, or so.

A gentleman came by in one of those pontoon boats everybody is currently crazy about. Just like me, he had been successful in snagging a few of the cutthroat who never got a college education. He had been watching me casting for a couple hours, so he didn't feel particularly threatened by my fly fishing prowess and felt comfortable enough to approach my boat. We talked for about three minutes before I exhausted my knowledge on fly fishing.

Then he shared with me a secret. There were some monstrous brown trout in the lake. He said they usually inhabit the reedy area over by the boat take out. He, himself, hadn't had any luck with those monsters, but he had heard a rumor.

I Went Down to the Willamette

The Willamette may not be the Wilson River with its spotty, but tremendous runs of steelhead, or even Eagle Creek, with even spottier runs, and the Willamette may not always be a pristine and beautiful river experience- but it's close to the house, and that counts for something to a man who is getting along in years and who's back nags on the longer runs in the Subaru. Besides, I'm probably not going to catch a fish, anyway, so I might as well not catch a fish closer to home.

I parked the car down the road from the McDonalds and walked down the blacktop path just opposite the yellow arches. This from a man who, when he was younger, laughed at hardship, teased those who could not stand the freezing cold of winter, and scoffed at the weak who could not or would not walk a half mile down to the river. Now, I park in town and fish within sight of the car a block from the McDonalds. I guess it serves me right for all the teasing and cajoling I did in the past.

Still, there are fish in the waters of the Willamette River near McDonalds- huge, mammoth, heavy bodied king salmon. When their respective runs are in, the salmon and steelhead fill the river to the max. There are also bank anglers, to the max, leaving hundred pound mono caught on rocks and snags, and there are about a million and a half boats stirring up the waters and making life along the riverside an occasional chore. I don't want a boat. I *want* to fish from the shore, so I put up with the waves nearly washing me off my feet, and I pity the other fishermen, because they are merely plunkers and don't know any better.

Few, if any other fishermen in the stretch from the Oregon City Bridge to Meldrum bar drift fish from the bank. I can't ever remember seeing another drift fishermen. Not that I blame them. It has never crossed their minds that drift fishing is even possible from the bank on such an expansive river.

They plunk. A plunker is someone who has purchased a huge and heavy fishing pole and implanted a gargantuan spinning reel on the already unwieldy device. So equipped, the plunker hauls back and throws a spin-n-glow and a poor misbegotten and smelly shrimp just as far out as he can get it. The strategy seems to be that farther is better regardless of the river, the bottom, the holding patterns of fish, or the lanes in which the fish travel. It's just toss and sit down to a beer and watch the tip of the pool-cue like fishing pole for any unusual or suspicious movement. There was a guy in the Bible that did something like that. He shot an arrow into the sky to see where it would land. It landed on the king, but the shooter would probably admit that he just got lucky.

I am not equipped mentally to join the ranks of bank plunkers or even plunkers in a boat- for that is what they are- they are just plunkers in boats. In the first place, their method of fishing is too sedentary for me. Even with a painful back, I cannot sit and just watch the tip of a fishing pole bobbing with the current. Besides, like I said- I'm probably not going to catch a fish, anyway, so why not wade in the water a little, and cast to several likely looking spots instead of just holing up in one spot and seeing what the arrow hits? Secondly, their fishing method is not productive. Thirdly, it hardly looks like fishing. Fourthly.., well, I just don't like doing it. I carry an eight foot Lamilglas steelhead rod that is light in my hand and easy to cast. A bait casting reel does just fine for me, and I'm too much of an artist to just lob out a gunk of shrimp and sit back on a rock. I yearn for small, intimate creeks where a long cast is sixty feet and most around twenty, but the Willamette is close and convenient.

In all fairness, one must remember that King Ahab fell to the plunker with the bow and arrow, so it is not an entirely unsuccessful method. It is just not my method.

Because it's so close to home, I got an idea that perhaps the edges of a big river, like the Willamette, might be fishable if one examines it in a different light. I took the Lamiglas down to the river near the McDonalds and looked for a fishy looking stretch of water up against the bank. Found one right off, too. It was easy with a little imagination. I just pretended that the river was not half a mile wide but only a hundred feet across- that way, the little ripple alongside my bank made more sense. In smaller creeks and rivers, I had fished a lot of little chutes like the one near McDonalds, and this one on the

Willamette had been there for years right under my nose, but I didn't see it because I was always looking out into the river and wishing there was a way for a man with a bait casting reel to get out there with the boats. I was thinking like a plunker, like the man who shot the arrow.

The fishermen in boats looked strangely at me as I threw my line so close to shore, but I knew a familiar looking little riffle when I saw one. The bank plunkers ignored me. They had no idea even what I was doing. Neither reaction bothered me. I just rigged on a spinner, that I had designed some thirty years earlier, slipped on a shot of lead, and presented an artful spot-on cast to my designated target area. The hole is a deep tail out right off the bank near the McDonalds. The weight took a five count before it hit bottom. As I began my slow retrieve, the spinner bobbed deep along the bottom keeping the tip of my Lamilglas vibrating to an enticing beat. I cast again.

There are only four tricks to fishing for salmon and steelhead; fish when the fish are present; fish a lure that the fish like; find a piece of water with just the right depth and current; and be absolutely on or very near the bottom. Do these things, and you can catch large fish. But, only one out of a hundred fishermen (probably a lot fewer than that) can recognize a good run with the correct depth and current, few know what lure will catch a fish if there are fish in the river, and even fewer will then be able to cast the lure and retrieve it at just the right speed and at just the correct depth. Very few fishermen can do all these things. And those that can- sure don't want to fish down by the McDonalds.

I don't want to stretch this metaphor too thin, but those bank plunkers get lucky every once in a while. Even the fella in the Bible hit the king's ankle with the arrow and killed him. So, it is possible to catch fish plunking from the bank- it's just that I find it incompatible with my personality.

I didn't touch a fish for the first hour. Every few casts, I would step downriver and begin plying the waters further down- always trying to quickly place my spinner on the bottom, keep it spinning at just the correct speed, not snag on the bottom of the river, and maximize my drift so as to cover as much water as possible in each cast. It is a highly productive technique that I have honed to a pretty sharp degree of expertise. I *should* be good at it. I've been fishing exactly the same way since the late 70's. That is a long time for honing, and while it doesn't take much practice to shoot an arrow into the sky and kill a king, it takes a bit of experience to successfully fish for steelhead and salmon down by the McDonalds on the Willamette.

When I reached the bottom of the drift, I turned and started back up. About half way up the drift, I noticed a funny and peculiarly attractive stretch of water below me that I hadn't noticed my first time through the drift. On the next cast, I free spooled a few feet of mono when the spinner reached that funny little stretch. The river looked like the current slowed nearly imperceptivity, and perhaps the water was a just a bit choppier, there, than the surrounding drift. The fish took the spinner with a jolt and went skyward two feet out of the water. So did I. It's like that sometimes. I get nearly mesmerized by the endless repetitions of casting, stepping up river, casting, stepping up river. The fish startled me. It also threw the hook.

It didn't matter one bit to me that the fish threw the hook. I had proved that if the river was studied and methodically examined with an experienced eye, fish could be caught without trying a desperate shot to kill the king. I didn't kill Ahab; I just hooked him in the mouth and let him go. It's called catch and release.

Just before leaving the river, I determined to try where the little chute I had been fishing spilled into a larger and quieter eddy. In a smaller river, the beginning of the quieter water would have been ideal. It looked fishy. On my first cast, I pulled up a twenty foot section of hundred pound mono. On my second cast, I lost my rig to another bunch of mono left behind by a plunker with a pool stick for a fishing pole.

When I got home, ten minutes later, I told Betsi how I had hooked a steelhead down by McDonalds, but that the fish threw the hook on its first jump. Betsi is pretty pragmatic and understands the deeper things in life. She went out and searched the car for a Big Mac wrapper.

Work called me away for a few days, and when I returned to the river I parked south of the McDonalds and walked down the path to the river. Just as my waders got wet, a big roan colored sea lion turned in the drift not twenty feet away. A smart man would have spun on his felt covered soles and gone elsewhere. I wasn't smart. Never have been. I also resisted the urge to fill that sea lion with lead. Instead, I fished that drift every way to Sunday, and never touched a fish. I didn't see anyone else touch a fish- except that I did see the sea lion with one about mid span out in the river.

A plunker engaged me in a discussion about fishing, and we agreed that it was a little early in the year for salmon, but the weather was so nice that we just had to go fishing. I looked up and down the river. There seemed to be about a hundred of us who just had to go fishing because of the sunshine and cool breezes. The salmon weren't there yet in significant numbers, it being the first part of April, with no dogwood trees in bloom, but we had to try. There's an old husband's tale, in this neighborhood, that the salmon don't show until the dog woods bloom. It's true, too.

One day a few years ago when I had a boat, I took my brother Harold out on the Willamette River near McDonalds. We fished all morning with nothing to show, and then the sun came out. One second it was dark, dreary, and dismal. The next, the clouds parted, and out came the sun. Then the most amazing thing happened; the sturgeon began jumping. I had never seen sturgeon jumping. Once in a great while one single sturgeon might jump, and it's a thing to take in, but all the sturgeon? People look kinda funny at me when I tell this story, so it's quite a relief to write it down where I don't have to see the looks of disbelief on so many faces all at once.

You see, sturgeon aren't just fish. They are

big fish. I mean, really big. I should italicize the word. You can't even keep one until they are four feet long! Those fish are monsters, literally. The sturgeon in Oregon City are white sturgeon. There are only three places in the world where white sturgeon inhabit a river, and the Willamette near the McDonalds is the only one in the western hemisphere! And Betsi thinks I only go to the Willamette for the cheeseburgers. (If it isn't true- that bit about being white sturgeon only in Oregon City- don't bother writing me. That statement looks good in print, anyway.)

 Back to Harold. Six foot sturgeon were jumping clear out of the water and splashing like whales! Ten foot sturgeon were jumping out of the water and splashing like.., bigger whales. It was a sight to behold! Harold was quite a guy, really, but he wasn't much for being in boats, and he wasn't wearing his life vest, and he was a bit edgy *before* the sturgeon began jumping. He looked at the sturgeon jumping, his jaw dropped open, and a few indefinite syllables were muttered. I, on the other hand, was in heaven. Sturgeon jumping! Drown me. I didn't care. Kill me. Who cares? Sturgeon jumping all around me showing their spiny back and large, stupid looking faces, their eyes all bugged out.

 Harold's face turned white, and he simply said, "Go in."

 Perhaps if I had owned a bigger boat I would have argued with him. I went in, but I made him pay for the burgers.

 A week later I was on the river with my daughter Jennifer. She was ten at the time. We started up by the old bridge and just drifted with the current trailing a couple worms. That's a fun way to fish with children. They don't have to know much. All they really have to do is hold the pole and wait for some action. On the Willamette, the sky is nearly the limit trailing a couple worms- salmon, steelhead, whitefish, sucker fish, bass, sturgeon.., and ten pound carp. She caught the carp. You should have seen it! It was a ten pound, thirty inch goldfish! It was incredible. It looked ever so much just like a little gold fish in a clear see-through bag at the county fair, only this fish was ten pounds with scales as big as nickels!

    We took the fish home to show Jennifer's mother. When we pulled that fish out of the car at the house, the fish was still sucking air and making the cutest little squeaky sounds. Mom was not impressed. In fact, her mother was kind of upset by the whole smelly fish thing and all way up to the porch was still making sucking air noises and the cutest little squeaky sounds. I buried it under the cherry tree. The fish, of course.

    The best day I ever had on the Willamette River was when a friend of mine phoned his father in Arizona.
    That day, I was not fishing down by the McDonalds. I was at Meldrum bar which is closer to Burgerville. I try to keep geographical references pertinent.
    The salmon were definitely running, so I had that covered, and I was still armed with my personally designed little spinner, so all was well on that score. I know how to throw that spinner. I fish it more like

eggs than a spinner. A slow, gentle, floppy retrieve really turns steelhead and salmon on. Well.., to tell the truth, that kind of retrieve really turns steelhead on, but with salmon you need to also bump 'em right in the nose. Salmon on the Willamette are a little dour. The best way to catch them is to snag 'em, but some politician in Salem made that illegal, so we salmon fishermen have been reduced to snagging them pretty much near the mouth and then doing a little rearranging when the fish comes to the net.

The story begins in church the day before I actually went to the river. I was amazing a young assistant pastor with stories of large fish, and he was absolutely star struck. Well, he should have been star struck, but after a while he began to doubt. I regaled him with tales of ten pound steelhead caught five minutes from the church. Twenty pound silvers slanted his eyes and made him look sideways at me. So, I told him about the fifty-four pound Chinook salmon I caught on the Clackamas River up past the Safeway. That pretty much did it, with him, and he found other things to do with his morning.

On Meldrum bar the next morning, I was having trouble finding a spot of water wide enough to cast into. Plunkers lined the bank. It was cold, and they had fires going. Several fishermen (rather.., plunkers) were standing around hot red barrels with flames leaping skyward. Dozens of poles were unattended with their tippets bobbing in the current. I took the scene in, nodded to several plunkers warming their hands at the fires, and scanned the river bank for a spot to cast.

Finally, I located an area and walked up to

stake my claim. When the fishermen on both sides took in my bait casting reel and spinner they gave audible grunts of dissatisfaction and alarm. I didn't blame them. It was like being a bicycle rider at the Nascar starting line. One of the plunker's opinion was that casting a spinner would foul his line. I couldn't blame him. He didn't know if I could cast or not, and quite frankly there wasn't much of a open area between a plunker up river and the next plunker down.

      The first cast, a sixteen-pound salmon opened his mouth just as my spinner was coming by, and I fair hooked it in the mouth on the lower lip. Plunkers down river scattered from the heat of the fires to grab their poles and reel in. When a big salmon takes hold on a river bank- an angler had better be prepared for running down river, because you sure can't convince such a large fish to let you stand in one place. He took me down to the shallow water near the boat launch, and I pulled him up onto the round flat stones. It was a beautiful winter day. The sky was clear and blue. The river was sparkling in its winter prime. Eagles flew overhead. I bashed his head with a rock.

      When I carried the fish back to the spot where it had been hooked, the plunkers moods had done a 180. It was lost uncle Harry coming back from the wars. My back was slapped, my hand was pumped, and the fish was measured. Twice. One of the guys had a spring scale he had purchased across the road at Fisherman's Marine Supply, and he held the fish up with the hook of the scale in the fish's gill. The scale read six pounds at first, eighty-two if the guy jiggled it just right, but about nineteen in between, and it looked to be about that, to me, so we called it good. I laid the fish down away from the bank, but close enough to keep an eye on it, and went back to my narrow span of water between the plunkers above and the plunkers below.

I did not catch another salmon on my first cast. Took me three! This one was twenty-six pounds, and I beat on it with another Indian smasher tool.

I'm nothing if not a braggart, so I headed over to that assistant pastor's house. When I pulled into the driveway, he was standing outside talking on the phone to his father in Arizona. I opened my door and walked to the trunk of the car without saying a word.

"My father says," yelled the assistant pastor, "that the rivers, here, don't have fish that big."

I just plunked 'em both down onto his driveway. Blood splattered everywhere.

The Willamette may not be the Wilson River with its spotty, but tremendous runs of steelhead, or even Eagle Creek, with even spottier runs, and the Willamette may not always be a pristine and beautiful river experience- but it's close to the house, and that counts for something.

Salmon Fishing

I had the supreme pleasure and honor to be raised in a small town with a cold, factory sounding name, Bremerton. Doesn't exactly strike a pose does it? It's a Navy town, with a capitol N. In the fifties, there were upwards of fifty thousand shipyard workers in that town. Everyday, those blue collar workers, who made Navy ships and saved the world during the last big war, reported for work at 0723, and everyday, they walked out the gate at 1643 hours, 7 a.m. and 4:43 in the afternoon, respectfully. There was the loudest horn you ever heard at four forty-three in the afternoon! It was loud, and after many many years it also became something sweet to my ears. Today, I would give a bit of my net worth to hear it blow again. In about 1973, some little girl's mother complained that the horn kept waking up her napping little tyke, so the horn was sequestered down to a shameful blip, blip and a low wheeeeeeewoo. When I returned from my first few months working in Portland, it was quite a shock *not* to hear the horn bellowing loudly. With the volume turned lower, it sounded like a frog with a stick in its mouth. Admittedly, before they lowered the volume, you could hear the old horn half way to Seattle, but then that's what it was there for. The Lady's point was two fold; she wanted her children to sleep a few more minutes, so she could watch Jeopardy, or something; but her other point was that all those fifty thousand workers were government employees, and while it was nice for everyone in town to hear the loud old horn and be notified that the shipyard traffic would soon be starting up- did anyone ever have to tell a government employee that it's quitting time? It should be remembered, here, that *I* am a retired government employee, so.., I know what she was saying. That old horn, however, was an auditory historical landmark. It had blown, and blown proudly, for a time span that only the Almighty knows, and he isn't telling, because He likes us to do our own research. My father, and about half the other old timers in town, if the truth be known, had a real health issue when that horn was reduced to a booble, a hoot, and a wheeeew. Dad found that after all those years listening to the real thing, his stomach just wouldn't work properly on the new wheez and a cough. Life marches, er.., growls on.

  Bremerton is nearly an island, all but just a pinch of land keeps it from being entirely surrounded by salt water. All that salt water was a wonderful playground for a few boys growing up who didn't have to listen to horns to be regular. There were things to do on Kitsap Peninsula- king salmon, silver salmon, steelhead, rock cod, halibut, sea bass, killer whales, porpoise, octopus, oysters, clams. That water was a smorgasbord. Dad kept saying that we should have been there twenty years before, but I thought it pretty wonderful in my day.

One wonderful summer afternoon, dad and mom packed us five boys in the old green Oldsmobile and we headed for Kitsap Memorial State Park, up by Hansville. When we pulled into the park, there were about ten girls, in the park, riding horses back and forth, back and forth. Dad and mom thought that looked pretty pointless, but we boys did not share their particular point of view.

After we picked an amiable looking picnic bench and fire pit, dad smiled broadly and suggested we boys take the trail down the beach and pick up some clams. For some reason, we boys had lost our interest in clams. Dad was pretty much dumb founded, at that, but he finally talked us into following along behind him with the large five-gallon pail. The beach was deserted, and we began just reaching over and picking clams up off the mud or raking the clams with a garden rake. It was that easy! Dad was humming a tune and smiling. He was in heaven. I guess with us boys having fun with him down on a beach it was like the good old days when everything was better. Looking back on it through the lens of time, since, I have to admit that it was paradise, and we boys did not even know it. We pretty much filled that bucket about half way to the top in about the time it would take those girls to ride the loop around the park twice. We filled that pail, and Dad just continued smiling and humming.

We must have made kind of a funny looking procession hiking that winding trail up to the park-dad leading the way smiling and humming like some mad pied piper, and we boys following along toting that heavy pail full of clams. I remember the thick wire handle cutting into the palm of my hands. When I couldn't carry, any longer, we would set the pale down and rest. Harold was in the front (Harold was always in the front of everything) and Tommy and I switched off on the back handle. Either Tommy, or I, would beg to set the pail down and rest, and Harold would pretend that he wasn't tired.

Finally, we three boys topped the rise and could see that the girls were still riding their horses back and forth. Tommy started smiling and humming a tune like he was in heaven. Dad wondered what was with that, but when he saw Harold buddying up to a horse and rider, he caught on real fast and carried the pail the rest of the way to the fire.

Clams are pretty easy. We filled the bucket with fresh water and put it over a wood fire. When the clams got hot and opened up, we dipped 'em in butter and ate 'em! For fifty years, we boys talked about those clams. On mom's death bed we talked about those clams, and the sunshine, and the fun of being all together at Kitsap Memorial Park. Tom swears that he does not remember those girls on horses, but thinking back on it- his wife is usually around when we are talking about the good old days.

Clams and girls on horseback was not all there was at Kitsap Memorial. In the water there were, and still are today, world sized king salmon. Biguns. But you don't put in at Kitsap Memorial; you go around the tip of the peninsula to a spit of land called Point no Point.

Point no Point was named by the Indians, who in the tradition of northwest Indians kept their names simple and to the point. When the tide is out, there is a very long and prominent sand spit jutting out into Puget Sound. The spit aims directly at the southern tip of Whidbey island, three miles in the distance. When the tide comes in, the water covers that spit, and there is no more point of land. Kinda like when the magician pulls a rabbit out of his hat and then the rabbit disappears in a cloud of smoke. Point no Point is like that. It doesn't sound like much in print, but just watching the spit appear and disappear makes people laugh.

We found that when the tide was in and the water was deepest, the fish were rather difficult to locate. We would ply back and forth across the current hoping to locate the run. But when the tide would change and start to run out, the current would rip across that sand spit like a large and mighty river, and the fish would line up on the down current edge just like fish lie below a large rock in a river current. It was then, when the current was turning and running, that we would find some incredible fishing opportunities.

I remember being about ten years old the first time we went to Point no Point. I sat in the boat in utter amazement at the wide open and expansive, horizon to horizon- nothing but water- like- forever! Way off in the distance, Whidbey Island loomed with its huge, white sandstone cliffs. Closer, but still tiny, my eyes clung to the houses that lined the road by the boathouse where we had launched. Water and more water, and the smell of salt, fish scales and fish guts, the exhaust from the six horse Johnson outboard, seaweed, and more fish smells. All those smells just mingled together. It's almost as if I can smell them now. The boat was never still. It would bob and dip and rise and slide from side to side. It's erratic jogging back and forth, up and down, side to side, mixed with the smell of gasoline and fish guts was really interesting. I was usually sick the entire day, but I loved it.

Dad plug cut a six-inch herring. Plug cutting is an easy process but one that demands a tricky little angle cut. You take a very sharp knife and slice across the neck of the herring. It's the angle of the cut that is critical to the spin of the herring. The first hook goes just through the shoulders of the herring, and the second hook passes through the tail. The line between the front hook and the second is just a mite shorter than the length of the herring, so the herring has to kink up some. Both the angle of the cut, and this kinking up, is what give the herring its characteristic spin in the water. Get the spin right, and mom cooks salmon for dinner. Get it wrong, and that herring just spins and spins until it starts to fall apart and becomes something hideous to look at for both fish and man.

The herring was tied to two feet of hundred pound mono- big, thick, heavy stuff that reminds me, now, of line I use in the edge trimmer on my lawn. Two feet above the herring, dad always tied on a ten-inch bright and reflective flasher. All this was followed by sixteen pulls of line, and the pole was held tight. For years, dad would tie his prized fishing poles to the oar locks or the seats, because he just could not get comfortable with three little boys promising not to let go of his prized salmon poles and reels. It was all great fun, but years later I would tie my *children* to the boat.

Fishing with dad was always great fun. When a fish would hit, the pole would take a drastic tug straight down- maybe that pole would dip a foot. Sometimes, it would dip like that two or three times. My first tendency was, and still is, to grab the rod hard and yank it back to set the hook. In dad's boat that was frowned on. "Give it some line, Lenny," dad would say. So I would pull out six more pulls and lean toward the fish in expectation. Everyone in the boat would be leaning forward. Finally, after about six months, that Chinook salmon would pull long, hard, and deliberate. Then dad would yell, "Set the hook!" Still, though, I was a ten year-old boy, and although I gave it my all- setting the hook never equaled dad's. But it worked well, often enough.

Those fish would go absolutely berserk, once they realized they were fighting in a life and death struggle. Imagine that? First, they would run. Line would just sizzle off the reel and actually blister my thumb. Dad would turn the boat around and follow a really big fish, but usually, he just let off on the gas and we would bob around with a little boy pumping his rod up and down trying desperately to gain some of that sizzled off line. Those fish! Many of them were well over thirty pounds. The cultural term for a twenty pound salmon was shaker; they were so small (compared to a salmon of fifty to a hundred pounds) that people would joke about shaking them off the line so as not to be bothered with such a small fish. I never saw anybody really do that, but that was the ever prevalent joke. "Twenty pounds? Nice fish, boy, but we usually shake fish like that off. Why bother with the small ones?"

There was some justification in that philosophy where many of the fish were fifty pounds, and I myself some many years later, had on a true, blue, hundred pound king. As I remember it- back when you didn't even need a license to fish for salmon in salt water- because it was a God given right and not something the State of Washington bequeathed, the average fish was thirty pounds. Many were much larger- at a time when I probably weighed in at sixty!

Netting a monster of a fish was always another fun part of the adventure. Dad would be tending the motor, so mom often handled the net. Mom would get a little excited. The fish got a little excited, and I was always coiled up like a spring about to break. One of us boys would swing the fishing pole over, so mom could take a swipe at the fish with the net. When that fish would feel the aluminum frame of the net, they would go a bit nuts! That king would be off again, like a rocket, and we would have to do the same thing all over again. Dad would just laugh and laugh. At the miss, mom would flop back down onto the boat seat, wipe away an errant strand of hair, and be all teeth and a grin. She was fun. If it was a really big fish, she might start shaking with buck fever, and her teeth would chatter.

One time, Tommy was just setting his plug-cut herring into the water when a fish hit. Standard operating procedures was to not let any line out, at first, just hold the rod directly out sideways from the boat to examine the action of the herring- to see how the herring would spin. Well, it must have been spinning well, because a silver salmon took that herring six feet from the boat in bright sunlight!

Tommy's silver was a frantic fight. I remember it, today. You cannot hook a salmon with six feet of line and bring it in. A heavy fish should break the line, or the rod, but we were all lucky this time. All but the salmon. Dad yelled, "Throw the freespool! Throw the freespool!" and to dad's relief Tommy calmly flipped that little pin to let the line run out free and clear. That salmon jumped once, splashed us all, and took off for Whidbey Island. I mean, he did not like the way we looked! It was probably Harold who frightened him.

After Tommy was able to let out a few feet of line, he could battle that fish like all the others he had fought successfully. It was pump and reel, pump and reel, and then watch mom take a stab at it. Then it was pump and reel, pump and reel, and watch mom take a stab at it. She was hilarious. If she made a beautiful sweep and caught a fish in the net, she wasn't strong enough to do much of anything else, so dad would throw the Johnson in neutral and try to get across three boys to help mom pull in the fish. Trouble was, by the time dad got there, all three boys had usually managed to get in the way trying to help mom, and that put about five of us on one net, all crowded over on one side of the boat straining the stability of a little orange rented boat. We were all in heaven.

Not one time, did any of us boys fall in the water. We should have once or twice, but we did not.

We did rescue a couple men who were in the water, and many times we towed in a boat with a broken motor. Usually, the people we helped would be real friendly out on the water where their lives were on the line, but once closer to shore, reality and pride would hit them. Most never even said thanks. It might have been the tiny six horse Johnson outboard or the three kids, all wearing orange life vests, or it might have been the brightly painted orange boat. It became a little joke between dad and myself. We would tow some hapless angler for a mile and drop him and his boat at the boathouse- we would rescue people from water as bad and treacherous as the open ocean, we would tow a man and his wife and his dog to the only place he could get help for miles around- and he would not even turn around to say, "Thank you." I would look at dad, and he would smile.

    I went back to Point no Point a few years ago, and was amazed, yet again. Not much has changed, except the people and the fact that the rented boats aren't run down to the water on a train track off a dock twenty feet up in the air. Everything else is the same. The point still disappears when the tide comes in, and we stood in front of the lighthouse to watch the water. When the tide turned, we watched a man from the shore play a large, old Chinook salmon! So, the fish are still there. The boathouse is still there. You can rent a room in the lighthouse for about a million dollars a night. Tommy and I, and our two wives, walked up and sat down on the rocks in front of the lighthouse and just happened to sit down next to two people who had known Tom's wife when she was a little girl in Wenatchee. It was a fun day.

Dad and mom are gone, now, and so is Harold. Life is like that, and I miss them all but most of all, I probably miss Harold. We became great friends.

I thought about renting a boat and some fishing gear and going out for a king salmon, but Betsi suggested that I should just let that memory lie. Besides, with the movement of the water, the smoke from the outboard motor, and the smell of fish guts- I'd just be sick again.

Point no Point was named by the Indians, who in the tradition of northwest Indians kept their names simple and to the point. When the tide is out, there is a very long and prominent sand spit jutting out into Puget Sound. The spit aims directly at the southern tip of Whidbey island, three miles in the distance. When the tide comes in, the water covers that spit, and there is no more point of land. That is a sight to see. Give me a call, and we will take the drive.

Mukilteo

Mukilteo is a small town northwest of Seattle. It's one claim to fame is the ferry that takes people to Whidbey Island. A few years ago, the point was populated by the Snohomish Indian Tribe. That was a few years before my time. I'm not sure the Snohomish Indians really had a word for what we, today, call time. They had seasons, and more seasons, but until Captain Vancouver visited them and started the tribe on the way to the wonders of civilization, they could only relate to past experiences by grunts and smiles. They had no word for yesterday or tomorrow. A wife would say, "When are you coming, home, Harry?" and the Indian chief would just smile. Come to think of it, life hasn't changed that much-except the Indian wife couldn't phone the bum up every five minutes and bug him about coming home on time, not driving if he'd been drinking, staying away from other women, and such.

My brother Tom phoned and said that the salmon were running at Mukilteo, and why not come up from Portland and try it tomorrow? Fortunately, white men have a name for that tomorrow thing. "Sure!" I answered and immediately got my packing on.

Tom had this great idea. We could rent an outboard motor from the 7 Eleven and then rent a boat at the marina. It seemed easier to me if we just rented both from the marina, but he had heard that the 7 Eleven motors were only five dollars a day, so why pay the thirty the marina charged? Something didn't ring quite true with his story, but I agreed. I would have agreed with anything to go salmon fishing, but since dad was still alive I made Tom promise not to tell him we rented a motor from the 7 Eleven- for some indefinable reason it seemed a little sacrilegious to rent a motor from a Pakistani named Kevin to try for such a nearly holy quarry.

  I showed before light and loaded Tom and his coffee into my truck and we made the short trip to the dock. There was no problem with the motor. I think the Mukilteo 7 Eleven must be the only 7 Eleven with three or four outboard motors next to the ice machines, out front. Tom said he would spring for the boat if I got the motor. What he didn't tell me was that he was going to put a few donuts, a couple chocolate milks, half a dozen of those long meat sticks and some lottery tickets on the same tab as the motor. "While you already have your card out..," he muttered.

  Across the street at the marina a couple twelve year olds rented us a sixteen foot wooden boat and slid us down the ramp into the cold and frigid waters of Possession Sound. The boat hit the water just as the sun came over the hills to the east- and just as the Whidbey Island Ferry decided to pull away from the dock.

  Tom said something about wishing he had brought his coat, just as the wash from the ferry tried to roll us. "You didn't bring your coat!" I yelled at the same instant that the ferry sounded her enormously loud horn, and a strong wind from the north kicked up spray into our faces. I cranked the motor to starboard, hit the gas and dove directly into the squall. It was that, or be swamped. That move, however, took the boat directly into a chop that was difficult to believe. The boat rode to the top of one swell, crested, and dropped down the backside of the huge up swell. Golden light from the newly risen sun played off the rocks and seaweed on the bottom of Possession Sound! Tom yelled something about his coat not being that important, and something else that sounded a lot like a prayer. The only thing to do was to crank the throttle full out and hope there would be some water down there, when we got to the bottom of the swell. There was. We hit the bottom of the swell, splashed more water all over us and miraculously shot out of the chop into the relatively calm of the water beyond. Tom was still praying when I found a second to look at him. He was also a mite wet from all the spray.

"Cheer up," I yelled to him. "I brought my coat, so I won't be cold."

Tom just did what he always does best in a pinch. He smiled.

Out of the chop, I maneuvered the boat to port so we could run along behind the ferry to get to the south of the point where all the salmon fishing was going on. As we bobbed over the last of the ferry's wake, I reached over and picked up my Lamiglas and hit the free spool. The line went out ten feet, twenty feet, and then- Whammo! Five minutes out from the marina, just past the ferry, hugging hard around the point, and the first salmon was eager to bite!

The Chinook hit solidly and ran at the first bite of the hook. The salmon's run gave me some pause, for I was using my Ambassador steelhead reel. There's just not the line capacity needed for boat fishing large king salmon on water more like the ocean than anything else. The reel is marvelous along the bank of a river, but in an open boat with fish that could run off a hundred yards of line, as a matter of course, I was afraid that I might run out of mono. I tightened up more than usual and forced the fish in.

"Too bad you don't have a net," stated Tom.

"We have a net," I countered. "It's on the floorboards behind you."

"I have a net," he said flatly. "Did you bring a net?"

I didn't answer for a few minutes. I had my hands full. When the fish was close, I turned to look at Tom.

"I remembered the net," he said with a smile. "You remembered your coat."

The salmon came to the side of the boat, and Tom (bless his heart) picked up the net. As I swung the fish over to him he made one quick stab with the net and took the fish from the tail end- like a pro. The fish settled into the net. Tom just let it set there.

Now a freshly netted king salmon will lie quietly for a second or two- then sensing that there might just be a way of winning his freedom he will often commence to thrash a mite. I mean like it is pretty difficult for a strong man to hold a net when a big king starts thrashing. And there was Tommy just holding the fish without folding the net or bringing the fish into the boat.

"We can share the coat!" I yelled as quickly as I could. "We can share the coat!"

"That's only fair," said Tommy still smiling. He turned the net and with one deft movement lifted the fish and threw the net and all into the bottom of the rented boat. "Only fair," he repeated. "I mean, I will share my net with you, and you share your coat with me."

I pounced on the fish.

It was a good salmon of about sixteen pounds but only a shaker. Even though dad had said there was a time, when he was a boy, that fishermen would not keep a sixteen pound salmon fresh out of the ocean- that men would just shake the fish off so they could get back to fishing for *real* fish- Tom and I decided that dad was not a boy any longer, and would treasure that fish for dinner tomorrow night. He did.

I pounced on that shaker and beat it over the head with a wooden mallet supplied for just such a purpose.

Then I gave Tom my coat. His lips were turning blue.

Other boats around us were catching fish, so I put the motor in gear and free spooled my little spinner. It wasn't ten minutes before I hooked another, and Tom was kind enough to both net the fish and loan me my coat for a few minutes.

It was like that through the early morning hours. I lost two fish but put two in the boat by ten, and then the bite died down. By then the sun was warm, and I threw my coat into a ball up in the bow of the boat. Tommy broke out the lunch and the junk he put on my tab up at the 7 Eleven. We ate most of the candy and the meat sticks first.

"Hope I catch a fish," said Tom.

I hadn't noticed that Tom hadn't hooked anything. I was so much into bringing in two fish and having two others on, that I hadn't even realized that Tom was just setting there with his pole bobbing in the current. "Can't believe it!" I remarked. "We are using the same gear, and I'm hooking 'em like crazy, and you aren't. Works for me, Tommy."

"Switch poles with me."

I didn't mind that. Both poles were mine, anyway. I designed the spinners twenty years before. I put on the magic reflecting tape. I tied the weights on. I did everything except let the line out for him, and he could not catch a fish to save his life.

We left the lines out and watched the tips bobbing with the current while we laid back against the gunnels and started in on the lunch Linda had put up for us. That was the life- bobbing along with the current, watching the tip of the pole as the line bounced along on the bottom of the bay. Not a care in the world, and we were together, we two brothers, salmon fishing on Puget Sound. Wish I was there now, and you were in your office writing a book in your pajamas.

They call it mooching when you just let the boat drift with the tide. You can cover an awful lot of water in a short span of time, and it is highly productive for catching salmon, rock cod, and ling cod. We drifted along until about one o'clock when Tom said that he couldn't stay out much longer.

Just at the moment- that very moment- Tom

said his schedule wouldn't let him stay out on the water more than another half hour, or so- another fish took my spinner. I set the hook and then sat back as if nothing had happened. We talked for a few minutes- all the time with a large fish on the line- without Tom knowing anything was going on.

"Well, I'll tell you what, Tom," I said matter of factly. "This has been one of the most wonderful days of my life. I miss you all the time, and wish I didn't live so far away in Portland and you in Seattle, but this day has made up for it a little bit."

He agreed.

"But, I'll tell you what, Tommy. You reel my line in for me, and I'll start the motor and head for the boat shed.

Tom reeled in his own line professing his disappointment in not catching a fish, but reveling in what a marvelous day it had been. Glorious didn't quite do it justice, he said. When he took my rod, I kept a straight face and turned away from him to start the motor. Before I had it chugging away, I heard him exclaim, "Fish on! Fish on!" That was fun.

When we were boys growing up and salmon fishing, Tommy was the champion, so he knew how to catch fish, and he knew how to bring them in. I readied the net and sat back to watch. It was a larger salmon than I had caught; that was evident from the start. The fish sounded. Tom cranked it up. The fish sounded again. Tom pumped it back up. Then the fish ran for the boat. Running towards the boat is classic king salmon strategy. They often run straight at the boat and pass under and keep on going. But Tommy had seen that before and just thrust the pole under water and followed the fish to the bow. Submerging the pole kept the line from catching on the bottom of the boat or motor. With Tom in the bow, that kind salmon took off again on a sizzling run straight northbound with our Yamaha tight on his six. He didn't have a chance.

I netted that fish for Tom, and it weighed in a few minutes later at forty-two pounds. Not bad for two boys who hadn't been salmon fishing for years and one boy who forgot his coat and thought they could rent an outboard motor for five dollars a day!

Even though the motor turned out to cost five dollars an hour, I would gladly pay much more than that for one more day in a boat with Tommy.

Mukilteo is a small town northwest of Seattle. It's one claim to fame, in my mind, is that its waters were kind to two boys who had grown up and were allowed to have one last memory of salmon fishing together.

Funny Things and Weird Things

Once, I saw a man fishing on Eagle Creek with no clothes on. I don't know too much more about this story except that it was in the first hole above the Corner Hole. I did a quick about face and did not stop at the office, or call the police, or ask him if he needed any help. Clearly, any man who would stand in the middle of Eagle Creek not wearing a stitch of anything solid is beyond help.

One lovely spring morning, I was startled to see a buck deer swimming down the middle of Eagle Creek. He went straight through the slot below One O'clock Rock and over the lip of the tail out. I watched him as he waded through the shallow water until he went out of sight where that old blue Toyota used to be in the water for two or three years. He was a good looking buck, but I did not cast to him.

On the Clackamas, one spring day, I

misjudged the weather. A day that started out mild turned down right hot. At noon, I stopped just below the old Park Place Bridge and brought out a peanut butter sandwich. I was without any water, and that peanut butter stuck in my throat like a hot load of concrete setting up. Man, was I thirsty! I remember saying, "Lord, how I would like a cold beer!" Instantly- like I mean right that moment- a Budweiser can floated down the Clackamas, settled in the little eddy made by my two booted feet in the water, and stopped in the Clackamas River right between my legs. Still, I was clueless. "Oh, yeah!" I replied, to Him Who Sends All Good Things, "but it's probably empty!" It wasn't empty, and in a second neither was I!

On the upper Clack, just above Lazy Bend Campground, I was standing on the one and only rock in that stretch of the river. That rock is about five feet high- pretty easy to climb onto but just high enough to make for a difficult and clumsy dismount.

I was on that rock, early one morning, when a muskrat and her six little ones came swimming down the river hugging my shore. It worried me some, when they all decided to go ashore right at my rock. A few of the babies went on one side of the rock, and a few on the other. The mother started around the down current side of the rock, and then she looked up and spied me on that rock. Now, I stand about six feet tall, and that muskrat was only about ten inches high all stretched up with her back hunched, but she made one hideous and scary looking opponent when she bared her teeth and hissed. Luckily, she hurried off to find her little pups hiding in the brush. I decided that I needed to find a taller rock.

On Lake Washington, I was casting a red and white Daredevil from the shore one beautiful and sunny morning. I was in the Marines, at the time, and was assigned as a training officer in a squadron of cargo planes at Sand Point Naval Air Station. I was having a great time casting and casting. I never saw a fish, so I guess I was just casting, not really fishing. In those days, I had a spinning rod, and boy would a heavy spoon like a half-ounce Dare Devil really fly.

On one particular cast, I marveled at the monofilament line billowing up up and away- high up in the sky. Then I marveled at something else; one, lone seagull was on a direct line of flight for my arching fishing line. My eyes watched and gauged the fall of the mono and the flight of the bird. Closer and closer they came together. Closer and closer, and then- that dumb bird flew right into the monofilament. The hook caught the gull right in the shoulder.

I had no idea what to do. There was nothing I could do. The die was cast. All this happened in a few seconds, and yet it was taking so long to play out that my mind was working overtime. The shiny spoon stopped its falling arch and did a kind of tight little spiral motion. The bird, realizing something weird was happening, dove to his right.

If I had cut the line, right then, all might have been OK, but I had never been in that position before. I had never read anything like that in any fishing magazine. It was unchartered ground.., er.., air. The farther the bird flew to rid itself of the line- the closer the spoon worked up toward the bird. I knew what would happen when the bird and the spoon finally collided and I readied myself. The bird kept flying, the spoon kept getting closer- and then, finally, that spoon impacted the bird's shoulder and the hook took hold firmly.

    Now, this may not be a funny story, but it sure is strange. My reel started screaming, and my fishing pole started bucking. I had a big one on and had no idea how to play it or what to do with it. I had never read about the proper way to fight a wild and fighting seagull. At first, I tried to reel just to regain some of my precious line. Everything came hard on a Marines salary, and it had been difficult to justify the purchase of the fishing pole, reel and a bit of mono. How to find the cash needed for more line after only my first few minutes fishing?

    I wasn't making headway with the seagull, so finally I just gave up and snipped the line. Once free, that seagull flew dead east away from the pull of the line. Occasionally, way off in the distance I could make out a glitter from the shiny spoon. Then I started laughing. Who would believe my story? I laughed, and I laughed. Then, completely across Lake Washington- it must have been a half mile away- I caught one last flash of light off my one and only spoon. Then I laughed some more.

    In the mid-eighties, a couple put in at the old West Linn boat launch. The man owned a cabin cruiser- a boat with a bedroom and galley below decks. Off West Linn, the Willamette River is more like a lake; for miles and miles it is wide and calm water without a care in the world. After a while, the couple went down below. My grandmother called it sparking. The two lovers were oblivious to the rest of the world so caught up, were they, in generating a little spontaneous combustion.

Well, there is only about one thing to worry about drifting along *above the falls*. Above the falls is the operative, here, because if you have an above the falls, you must have a below the falls, and what is in between the above and the below is what got the two lovers. So, while the couple was inside building a fire, as it were, their boat was drifting nearer and nearer to Oregon City and the falls. In those days there was no cable stretched across the river just above the falls, because those in authority thought that no one could miss seeing such a terrible and fatal obstacle. I guess those authorities just were not thinking about fire safety.

My brother, Harold, and I were in my little fourteen foot runabout one lovely autumn afternoon. We were fishing below the falls, and as brave as Harold was he was growing edgy about getting any closer to the falls in Oregon City. In dry weather, those falls are of a good height, and the spray and foam and noise is tremendous. The noise gets tremendouser the closer one gets. I was having a little fun with Harold, but the truth is that we were getting so close to the falls that even I was getting a little edgy. From down below, those falls get scary as one gets closer. When you are down below, at the base of the falls, they are tall, imposing, and tremendouser than you could possibly imagine.

    From the back of the boat, I looked past Harold (who sat transfixed staring at the tremendouser sight) to the falls. Then I cranked my neck to look up at the water as it plunged over the top. When I looked away for a second, a boat rolled under the falls, and I heard Harold exclaim.

    In the great and cavernous pool below the falls, a boat surfaced and rolled over like some great, lost ghost ship, like some behemoth monster- and then rolled, again, out sight!

    That was it! I cranked the motor around and we were history.

    It seems that the two sparkers in the cabin cruiser never heard the roar of the falls, they never saw the spray kicking up, they were never aware of their impending doom. That cruiser sat in the bottom of the hole beneath the falls for months rolling up to the surface, every once in a while, to remind those in the land of the living not to play with other people's matches.

    That was a weird and incredible sight. I'm sure sorry it happened to those two love birds. To all who got an occasional glimpse of that boat rolling in the turmoil and spray from the waterfall it was a chilling sight. Wish I had never seen it.

    My brother, Tom, had a great shock, one day, when we were kids fishing with the family at Point no Point. We had been fishing since the break of day and had gotten no sleep the night before, so about two in the afternoon all of us were sleeping and dozing peacefully except Tom and dad who was operating the little six horse Johnson outboard motor. We were all holding our fishing poles but nodding off while the boat was lazily bobbing with the gentle waves. We were lulled into a lazy, hazy, kind of nap. Although the heart of winter, the sun had come out, and it was like summertime in a dream world.

Dad was concentrating on something to port when Tom noticed something strange at the stern of the boat behind dad. A giant eye had surfaced! Tommy swears that he tried to give out a yelp, but his tongue would just not work correctly. He froze.

The eye stared coldly at dad and then the great beast began to swim forward. When the eye was even with Timmy, he noticed that the whale was longer than the boat! It was an incredibly large mammal that righteously took Timmy's breath away. They stared at each other, the boy and the whale, eye to eye, and then the behemoth monster nosed down to disappear into the depths. Timmy swears that the whale's tale was fifteen feet behind the boat when it tilted up and the whale gently dove to the depths- mindful not to stir the waters in acknowledgment of the fragile craft. Timmy's estimation would put the total length of the whale to be around thirty-five feet in length.

Just as the whale disappeared into the dark waters off the Strait of Juan de Fuca, dad turned forward to see Timmy pointing in alarm. Dad's description was that of boy who had turned white with fear, red with alarm, and blue with dread- all at once and rolled up into a ball of scared stiff.

There really wasn't much for dad to do but watch the boy. So he did. Dad was quite a pragmatist, so he waited until Timmy finally calmed down enough to speak. Dad listened calmly without interrupting. Then dad related that the same thing had happened to him, as a young man, in nearly the same place- straight out from the boat house about a mile from Whidbey Island. He was glad that large whales still called Point no Point home.

"We are not the only ones searching for king salmon off the point," dad said, as he slowly lit his pipe. There was a strange gleam in his eyes. "Better not tell your mother until we are all safe and sound at home."

One August, our family of five boys, and mom and dad, loaded the camping gear into the Greenbrier and headed for Omak country- up in the very northeast corner of Washington State. Dad hadn't been there since he was a boy, and he was eager to see the lay of the land one more time.

It was the one wonderful vacation that all us boys talked about for the rest of our lives. It was the one last vacation we were all together on before Harold and Tommy grew up and left home and little brother Johnny was killed. We had the best time of our lives. We rode horses, searched for gold, got chased by a rattlesnake, and generally Huck Finned it across half a dozen lakes so pristine and unspoiled it was scary.

Then we hit Lake Wannacut. To us boys, it was just another lake to explore. To mom and dad it was flush toilets and showers for five boys who had been without for a week. To all of us in the family, it was heaven- but for different reasons.

The second day, an elderly couple approached

our camp fire and asked if we might have a boy who could row them around the lake the next day? They were likeable, and dad volunteered my younger brother, Johnny. That surprised me, because Harold was the oldest and was strong enough to row for about ten months without tiring. Tom was the intelligent and polite one, and people just naturally liked Tom, and he deserved it. Wesley was a bit young and had way too much fun wrapped up in his wiry, little body, and I just wanted the job too badly. As a boy I wanted everything too badly. I would just suck up to anyone. Pretty much like today.

  The next morning, Johnny met the couple at the docks and rowed the couple around the bend in the lake. I stood and watched straining my eyes until they went into the reeds first and then around the bend and out of sight. At lunch they returned and left again after a short bite and a nap.

  Johnny didn't say much- just that he rowed while the gentleman fished. His wife, it seems, was content to read and watch the sights.

  When the three returned at dusk, Johnny returned the boat to the lodge while the couple came, again, to our campfire. I didn't catch their names the first time we met, and when I asked again it turned out that they were from our home town of Bremerton and that they were the grandmother and grandfather of a boy I knew in school.

  In a couple days, our vacation ended, and we gave little more thought to the old couple.

  Back in Bremerton the next school year, I became fast friends with the elderly couple's grandson. One evening, I was at their table sharing dinner, when I remembered meeting the grandparents, and I related the story. Everyone at the table stopped, set down their dinner ware, and stared. It was obvious that something was amiss, but I no idea what?

My friend turned to his father who directed him to fetch a photo of the old couple. "Is this the two you are talking about?" my friend asked.

I took the photo and smiled broadly. "Yes. Great people. How are they?" I asked. "My little brother rowed them around the lake."

My friend broke the silence first. "Your little brother who was.., killed just recently?"

"Yes. In a traffic accident."

Everyone at the table was silent. I gazed in wonder from face to face. Finally, my friend's father spoke up. "Uh. You must be mistaken. That is a photo of my father and mother. They died in a car accident the winter *before* your vacation."

This is a true story. It happened just the way I wrote it, here, in this book of fishing stories. I've never figured it out, and have just learned to accept it as it is, and ever shall be.

I may have the highly unofficial record king salmon from the Clackamas River. The fish was 54 pounds. If you know of a larger reel caught fish on the Clack, give me a call. I'm in the book.

The fish took above Safeway- way up around the corner, but took me all the way back down river to that deep hole by the old water out take. I hauled it in and mashed it a big one, but not before the fish tried to bite me. It actually, turned its head, opened its mouth and took a swipe at me! I mashed it with a big ole rock and broke my finger in the process. Serves me right.

Once, I caught an eight pound fish just above Safeway. It had large lips and was chrome bright like a summer steelhead, but it had fairly large scales and no adipose fin. The fish took a large, deep and slow moving spinner fished in the deepest part of the river.

Who keeps records on trash fish? Isn't that funny? In the northwest, our rivers are so full of wonderful, fresh, large and glorious fish that we call anything without an adipose fin- trash. Bass have recently come into their own, but, still, most fishermen wouldn't give them the time of day. White fish are a wonderful fish in many places- even here in the states- but we pretty much ignore them and throw them back.

I have no idea what this fish was. It was up in the deep hole above Safeway- just in the tail out and directly in the current. It fought with all the ferocity and tenacity of an old shoe.

After holding the fish for a few seconds and admiring its beauty, I watched it fin back to obscurity.

Which is probably where this book is destined.

Thank You,

Len Collins

Made in the USA
Charleston, SC
30 June 2016